"Valley Christian High School is one of the finest schools in America. The *Quest for Excellence*™ should be lived out in every Christian school throughout the world. The 'Excellence Brings Influence'™ strategy and the *Quest for Excellence* journey of Valley Christian Schools is a model for every committed Christian. If we are going to reclaim our culture for the cause of Christ we must pursue a *Quest for Excellence*."

Josh D. McDowell, Author/Communicator

"It not only seemed impossible, it felt like a bad idea. Was I ever wrong! Watching what Cliff and the Valley Christian team accomplished through tireless effort, undying determination and unquestioned faith was life changing for me. The impossible was willed into existence and this "bad idea" is changing hundreds of lives each and every day. . . . starting with mine. This journey of faith is a must read."

Kevin Compton, Managing Partner, Kleiner Perkins Caufield & Byers /Co-Owner, Silicon Valley Sports & Entertainment and the San Jose Sharks

"When our son Tyler chose Valley Christian High School, Gayle and I were curious. What's so special about Valley Christian High School? By the 2002 football season we were cheering from the bleachers as Tyler quarterbacked the Valley Christian Warriors to the team's first of several Division I CCS championships. Most importantly, Tyler grew academically as well as spiritually in his Christian faith. I was especially impressed with the coaches, faculty and administration. Tyler caught the *Quest for Excellence* passion and so will the readers of this book. They will learn about the intriguing story of how Valley Christian came to be and that there is truly "something special" up there on top of the hill."

Steve Mariucci, NFL Head Coach

"Every Christian school educator should read *Quest for Excellence*. It is the most amazing story of God's provision for a Christian school I have ever read. I could hardly put it down."

Paul Kienel, Founder and President Emeritus of Association of Christian Schools International

"The NFL family life can be emotionally challenging. When we answered God's call to coach, we put our seven children in His hands and He has delivered. Valley Christian Schools' *Quest for Excellence* offers academic quality and an amazing athletic program that is so important to our children. They are flourishing! The book, *Quest for Excellence*, is for all who passionately seek to achieve what God intends!"

Mike Singletary, NFL Hall of Fame and San Francisco 49ers Assistant Head Coach - Defense

"Growing up within the hallways of Valley Christian High School still brings warm memories to mind. The solid relationships built with teachers and students . . . the dynamic education and stellar sports program . . . and the school's whole-hearted desire to equip each person with the knowledge of God's Truth underneath it all, has continued to impact me to this day."

Joy Williams, Provident/Sony BMG Recording Artist, 2006 Dove Nominee and 2001 Graduate of VCHS

QUEST
for EXCELLENCE™

Clifford E. Daugherty, Ed D.

TATE PUBLISHING, LLC

Published in the United States of America
by Tate Publishing, LLC
127 East Trade Center Terrace
Mustang, OK 73064
(888) 361–9473

ISBN: 1-5988643-1-9

060612

ACKNOWLEDGEMENTS

Sincere appreciation is expressed to several key people that helped make this book possible. Among many that helped, the following persons made significant contributions:

- Mike Annab read the book and made helpful comments during my initial drafts.
- Jane Rumph edited the entire book and helped draft portions of Chapter 22. She also transformed the book into first-person perspective from my third-person perspective and from a collection of self-contained stories into a historical, dramatic narrative.
- Kathy Keleshian greatly assisted in doing research to validate the historical accuracy of the book.
- Linda Skovmand and Judi Fuller greatly assisted in the final publication efforts.
- Werner Vavken recommended several heading titles.
- Pam Watson worked tirelessly to assist with repeated editing of the entire book.
- The Valley Christian School board members greatly supported and encouraged me in writing this book. Their faithful service to the Lord through the difficult journey of the school's development cannot be overemphasized.
- My loving wife, Kris, read and affirmed the accuracy of much of the book.
- Many friends read the pre-publication copy and made editing suggestions.

•Of course, this book would not exist if God had not worked supernaturally through hundreds of people including the VCS board, faculty, staff, parents and friends that gave of their time, talent and treasure to develop and bountifully bless the amazing ministry of Valley Christian Schools.

"Unless the Lord builds the house, they labor in vain who build it . . ." (Psalm 127:1).

DEDICATION

This book is dedicated to my loving wife, Kris, our son, Zane, our daughter, Kristin, her husband, Mike, and our grandchildren, Emily, Kaitlyn, and Jacob.

"As for Me this is My agreement with them," says the Lord. "My Spirit which is upon you, and My Words which I have put in your mouth, will not leave your mouth, or the mouth of your children, or the mouth of your children's children," says the Lord, "from now and forever" (Isaiah 59:21 NLV).

Clifford E. Daugherty, Ed.D.
May 3, 2006

TABLE OF CONTENTS

FOREWORD

WHEN GOD CAME TO
VALLEY CHRISTIAN SCHOOLS

BY ED SILVOSO

This outstanding book provides definite proof that God wants to show up on Monday mornings in the workplace—and in this case a school campus—as much, or more, than He does in religious services on Sunday mornings. *The Quest for Excellence*™ documents the journey of a Christian school—plagued by endemic struggles and financial, spiritual and corporate problems—from a place of quasi despair to total victory.

The story is even more remarkable because in spite of topnotch, godly leadership, intense prayer and plenty of good advice, the school was a sinking ship, and going down fast! Today, Valley Christian Schools owns one of the best, if not *the* best, private campuses in California with top of the line athletic, communication and academic facilities. Its teachers are well paid and very well cared for. Its sports teams have won coveted awards and championships. A school that had trouble attracting new students today has many more applicants than spaces, and its graduates are courted by leading universities with millions of dollars in scholarships awarded each year. Furthermore, in 2004 Valley Christian Schools was the only private high school in the state of California to receive the coveted Blue Ribbon School Award from the United States Department of Education.

But the story of VCS is definitely more than just positive cash flow, top of the line facilities and coveted awards. Those are just visible reflections of a much deeper and exciting reality. VCS is the story of board members, administrators, teachers and students learning to hear the voice of God in the marketplace in order to bring the presence and the power of God into the board room, classrooms, and especially into the office of its President/ Superintendent, Dr. Clifford Daugherty. Cliff summarizes the story of VCS very simply: "How God works through ordinary people to accomplish extraordinary achievements."

This is a story that my wife and I, along with our children, participated in personally in its early stages. Every Thursday, beginning in the mid 80s we met with four couples whose children were also enrolled at Valley Christian to pray for provision and protection for the school. We all believed in Christian education but deep down we struggled with unspoken doubts arising from the failure of VCS to provide the finest environment for our children to be trained for life.

Quite often we felt like Moses facing the Red Sea. In front of us we had waters that would not part, threatening to drown our children and us while Pharaoh's army was closing fast. Caught between a secular school system bent on destroying the faith of our children, and a Christian alternative too anemic to effectively equip them, we channeled our despair into intercession every Thursday evening. Two of the couples we prayed with were on the board of the school and the other two were leaders in different campus programs while I was the board chaplain. From such a vantage point we had a well-documented view of the many challenges facing the school and the demoralizing lack of progress in spite of the best intentions of godly teachers and praying parents.

As board chaplain I was often, in fact too often,

called on to help the board resolve what seemed like a merry-go-round of recurring problems: alcohol and tobacco on campus, teen pregnancy, interpersonal problems affecting students and faculty, uncertainty regarding VCS' facilities and the perennial lack of finances to make payroll.

Today, Ruth and I like to stroll the majestic new campus where VCS resides on top of one of the highest elevations in San Jose. Framed by the best high school football and baseball fields in the region, an Olympic swimming pool and an award-winning theater, it is hard to imagine how bleak the picture was just a few years ago. Not owning a campus, VCS, was forced to move from one rental property to the next like a spiritual gypsy.

In *The Quest for Excellence* ™ Cliff Daugherty eloquently describes and documents how God came to VCS, set up residence on campus and caused its leadership to live the supernatural life - naturally. He illustrates how many feeble streams were invaded and then flooded by His presence until they became united to form a rushing river. It washed away the debris obstructing God's will and purpose for a school that was founded to be a light on a hill, but was mired in a swamp of impotence.

Now, in light of such tangible success, it would be easy for uninformed observers to look for social, corporate and clever financial moves as the keys for such success. However, one critical point cannot, and must not be missed. VCS' success is the result of a spiritual breakthrough that came through discovering the reality of the spirit world, a new understanding that the heavens rule the earth, and that such problems on earth are rooted in the spirit world. This truth, coupled with a dynamic understanding of the role and effectiveness of intercessory prayer and the need to equip students as pastors on campus, has transformed VCS.

For my wife and me, the spiritual roots of the problems became evident during a sleepover that our youngest daughters, Evelyn and Jessica, had organized for their female classmates. After welcoming their friends and establishing some house rules, we went to bed. We were prepared for a long night since the girls were camped out all over the house with enough food and videos to last them an entire summer. However, around 2:00 AM our oldest daughters, Karina and Marilyn, awakened us requesting that we rush to the family room because something weird was happening!

There we found that one of the girls was exhibiting deep emotional problems. The roots went beyond mere psychological issues. They were spiritual in origin. It was something we had not seen in the USA, but we were familiar with similar experiences overseas. It was not a pretty sight to see this precious girl tormented in such a way while many of her classmates watched in utter perplexity.

At the same time, we were blown away by the spiritual courage of some of our young guests. One girl stood on a chair shouting instructions at the top of her lungs to the others: "If you know how to pray, pray. Whatever tool you have—praises, Scripture reading, singing, anything - use it right now because we are under spiritual attack!" A couple of the braver ones were praying with the distressed girl while others held hands, perplexity written over their innocent faces, while mumbling a spiritual SOS. What we found sent a powerful message to us: that the spiritual reality should not be ignored and that the students at VCS could be counted on to fight the good fight.

We identified the spiritual root and ministered to our afflicted guest. After she was set free by the power of God we spent time praying and counseling her bewildered friends. By 5:00 AM everybody was asleep, but Ruth and I had learned a very valuable lesson: to see what we have never seen—transformation at VCS—we would have to do what we had never done, because if we kept doing what we always did we would continue to see what we always saw.

The next day I made an appointment with Cliff Daugherty to make a bold suggestion. I knew what I was about to place before him was radical, but I had come to trust Cliff as a man of God, full of faith. He earnestly expected God to move VCS forward in spite of the many setbacks to date. I shared with Cliff that the spiritual dimension of the problem required the shifting of a major paradigm, the one dealing with our imperfect understanding of the spiritual realm. My book, *That None Should Perish*, was about to be released and in it I dealt with the reality of the spiritual realm, showing how often problems in the natural are a manifestation of unsolved problems in the spirit realm.

I explained to Cliff that the influence of the Enlightenment on the Western world has blinded many Christians to the spiritual dimension of life. This blindness, I explained, has prevented many from perceiving the reality and the influence of the spirit world. I invited Cliff to visit Argentina where a revival had been going on for several years, to gain insights that would enable him to shift paradigms and help prepare him to deal more effectively with VCS' difficulties.

In this book, Cliff shares the extraordinary circumstances that led him to accept my invitation and how upon his return from Argentina his eyes were open to the spiritual dimension and how he went on to act on this new understanding.

Cliff is one of the most anointed and effective

administrators I know, and when he sets his mind on a goal he always comes up with a most efficient strategy. Just a few weeks after the trip we found ourselves in a spiritual retreat with board members and administrators examining the Scriptures, studying biblical principles and praying a lot. The weekend climaxed with a time of repentance and rededication of each of us and of VCS to God's purposes. We made a formal invitation for Jesus Christ to come on campus as Lord over all.

A second retreat with the teachers had the same results. This awakening led to a presentation to the student body. The entire school began moving into a new spiritual reality. The turnaround began when Cliff felt that every student enrolled at VCS should have a fellow student praying for him or her. I must admit that even though I am a visionary and a dreamer, when I first heard Cliff's plan I had doubts as to its feasibility. From my perspective we had just begun to move into a new spiritual reality that was still too radical for many. Besides, I did not think there were enough intercessors in the student body to cover the entire school as Cliff proposed. But he had heard God—something that would become a trademark of his in the years ahead—and as he acted, the Lord validated his obedience with supernatural success. When an announcement was made for student intercessors to join the program, we were surprised to see how many enlisted. In fact, so many signed up that in just a matter of weeks, not months, everyone on campus was being prayed for on a regular basis.

The climactic moment came a couple months later during Spiritual Emphasis Week. I had been asked by Cliff to speak to the entire high school student body. As I walked into the assembly hall I was able to sense the improvement in the spiritual climate. It was obvious that something had changed, but how much I soon discovered.

A very attractive senior came down the steps to tell the audience how empty and needy she was inside in spite of the winsome image she had carefully cultivated. She went on to confess and publicly repent of sin and invited others to join her. Many did. Next, a popular football player took the floor to do something similar to be immediately followed by others.

When my time came to address the students I read Acts 1:8 and told them, "The Holy Spirit is speaking to many of you now. If He is asking you to accept Jesus Christ for the first time, or if you want Him to help you to better understand God's Word, or if you want to submit your life more fully to God's Holy Spirit, I want you to come forward and kneel on this gym floor right now." That was as far as I got with the message I had prepared. An unexpected spiritual stampede was in full progress.

In no time students, teachers and administrators were spontaneously on their faces on the gym floor crying out to God for forgiveness and spiritual empowerment.

While the principal was kneeling down in prayer a student began to pray for him with extraordinary boldness and anointing. I watched the surprised principal look up to find that the one praying for him was a student he had threatened with expulsion that same morning! What a dramatic turnaround!

The lunch hour—the most attended period on campus—came and went with no one leaving the gym. Afterwards Cliff said that if we ever needed proof that revival had come to VCS, we had it in the fact the students gave up their lunch to spend time in the presence of God. From that day on the spiritual climate at VCS changed for good. So much so that in a few years the school that was notorious for lack of finances, disciplinary problems, low enrollment, and no campus of its own, would go on to literally become a light on a hill. There were many battles still to win, but Valley Christian Schools had broken out of a spiritual POW camp and was now on the march!

The story of how this happened and the spiritual principles behind it is what this book is all about. Cliff tells the story as only he, a well-informed eyewitness, can since he was at the helm of VCS before, during and after VCS' transformation. But, ultimately, this is not about Cliff, VCS or any of us. This story is about God, and God is in the business of bringing healing and restoration to what the evil one once defiled. According to Luke 19:10, Jesus came to seek and save not just the lost, but also *that* which was lost. In my book *Anointed for Business* I define the marketplace as the combination of business, education and government, and I explain that Jesus' objective was to recover not just the souls of people, but the totality of what was lost through the fall in the Garden. Not only was our relationship with God lost, but also Christian education as well since sin prevented God from coming down in the cool of the afternoon to instruct His creatures as He had previously.

Today, on this side of the Cross, we know that Jesus succeeded in His redemptive mission, and as a result of such victory everything that was lost is now recaptured. Now it is our task to claim what Christ has already redeemed. *The Quest for Excellence*™ makes a compelling and convincing case for how this can and should be done, not just in Christian schools, but also in all of life.

Go on, read, and be inspired and equipped to see similar transformation come to your own sphere of influence.

PREFACE

There were five purposes in writing this book. They are:

1. To inspire and challenge readers to experience the supernatural life naturally in every walk of life. It is a message about how God works through ordinary people to accomplish extraordinary achievements.
2. To challenge Valley Christian Schools' students to understand that God established Valley Christian Schools to prepare them to positively impact our nation and the world through their personal Quests for Excellence.
3. To serve as a tool in the hands of teachers and parents to help students discover and develop their God-given talent to achieve their God-intended purposes.
4. To encourage and model the Quest for Excellence™ to new and maturing Christian schools.
5. To record the history of the development of Valley Christian Schools from 1986 until 2006 as an expression of thanks to God for His great works.

The book's dramatic but historically accurate narrative illustrates the "Principles and Practices," the "Core Educational Values" and walk of faith concepts that are included in the recurring text boxes that the reader encounters while reading the book. The content in the text boxes is taken from the last five chapters of the book. The reader may elect to ponder or ignore the text boxes while reading the book depending on which approach best serves the reader's purposes and reading style.

CHAPTER 1
"I'M NOT GOING DOWN WITH THE SHIP!"

No way! No how! No, thank you!

The very idea made me laugh out loud. My friend's suggestion that I consider applying for the open position of superintendent of Valley Christian Schools struck me as sheer folly. True, my years in education and my experience as founding principal of Los Altos Christian School, south of San Francisco, qualified me for the job at Valley Christian in nearby San Jose, California. But for the past year I had enjoyed a successful business in financial planning services, setting a company record for a first-year representative. Making a change was the last thing on my mind.

Besides, I knew Valley Christian Schools (VCS) was sinking in red ink. A few years back, VCS had grown from its 1960 founding into one of the largest Christian school systems in the United States. Its size had reached almost 1,400 students with five campuses. By early 1986, however, the impending loss of the high school's lease and conflicts with how to fulfill its mission threatened Valley's future. I heard about its declining enrollment, low salaries, deficit spending, and indebtedness.

"Not me!" I responded when my friend suggested I might be the right person for the superintendent job. "I'm not about to become captain of a sinking ship. The captain is always last to board a lifeboat after everybody else has abandoned ship—and VCS doesn't have enough lifeboats!"

I shook my head again. Taking charge of a foundering vessel just in time to evacuate the passengers was not an appealing career move at age thirty-seven. While I prayed regularly for God's leading and purposes in my life, I had no desire to court professional suicide.

Still, a familiar voice planted a disturbing question in the back of my brain. "If I sent you as captain of a sinking ship to evacuate women and children, would you go? Are you willing to be a professional martyr for Me? I gave My life to save yours."

Get A Heart Transplant

Allow God to transplant His thoughts, desires and purposes into your heart. Be willing to let go of previous assumptions and practices, even those long held. In particular, do not confuse personal or cultural preferences with timeless Christian principles.

"And I will give you a new heart with new and right desires, and I will put a new spirit in you. I will take out your stony heart of sin and give you a new, obedient heart. And I will put my Spirit in you so you will obey my laws and do whatever I command" (Ezekiel 36:26–27 NLT).

Chapter 22: 4

For a couple of months I tried to ignore the Lord's inquiry. Then while driving home after a fruitful day of work in May 1986, I sensed a divine presence enter my car with an arresting power. He seemed positioned in the back seat directly behind me, and began to speak: "I've blessed your work and you've enjoyed it, but I have another assignment for you. This business job is finished and a new work will begin. Take a rest—you'll need it—and prepare yourself for a great battle. I will be your strength and victory."

Awestruck, I managed to keep my Nissan Sentra on the road till I got home. That evening, I tried to explain the encounter to my wife, Kris. We wondered together: *Was this really God speaking? What did it mean?*

PUTTING OUT A FLEECE

I felt like Gideon as I questioned whether I had heard God's voice. Over the coming week my schedule bulged with the most promising appointments, but for the first time ever, not one sale closed. All my contacts responded enthusiastically to my pitch but needed to talk with a spouse or CPA or tax person before committing. Everyone asked me to return the following week.

A week without a sale grabbed my attention like the throbbing of the proverbial sore thumb. Kris and I pondered and prayed together. Taking a cue from Gideon, we laid out a fleece: I would keep the follow-up appointments, and if the situation repeated itself, we would conclude that God was speaking to us.

The next week brought an identical experience—no sales. Now we couldn't ignore the message. *"OK, Lord,"* I responded. *"If You're in this, You've got to take charge the whole way. What was that You said about a rest?"* Kris and I decided to pack our bags for a vacation. Borrowing a motor home from my parents, we hit the road and enjoyed a lovely trip through Yellowstone and the Petrified Forest National Parks. The weeks away never felt so refreshing.

When we returned, I made some phone calls. Bob Jaynes, an acquaintance who served as chair of the Valley

Christian Schools board of directors, did not sound too encouraging. Bob had enrolled his children at Los Altos Christian School while I served there as the founding principal. "I was impressed with how you ran Los Altos," he told me, "but the VCS board is looking for someone with K–12 leadership experience in a school system with a multimillion-dollar budget. Still, if you're willing to possibly waste a few hours of your time, I'm willing to risk setting up an interview with the board."

Board members, I learned, had interviewed four or five candidates but made no match yet. I arrived for my interview a bit early after the 110-mile drive from our home in Elk Grove, south of Sacramento. Kris and I had moved to Elk Grove to buy a home when I started my sales job. Pulling into a nearby restaurant parking lot, I sat in my car to pray. Thoughts formed about what a new superintendent should set as priorities of VCS leadership, and I got out a pen and notepad to capture them.

During the interview, one of the board members asked me, "What do you think should be the priorities of the VCS superintendent?" I pulled out my notepad and shared the thoughts that had just come to me. The directors seemed stunned.

I discovered later that my ideas matched the priorities of the board. Within a week or two, after checking my references, they offered me the job. Kris and I found a small rental home in San Jose, where we moved with our two teenagers: Kristin, 15 1/2, and Zane, 14. I started work on July 21, 1986.

A CRIPPLED SHIP
In my new office on the junior high campus, I held my head in my hands as the number and size of this leaking "ship's" holes began to overwhelm me. Valley Christian

Schools faced a $420,000 deficit for the coming academic year. Tackling this debt looked as hopeless as bailing out the Titanic with an ice bucket. Enrollment had shrunk to about 1,000 students on four campuses: the Calvary and Howes elementary, the junior high Ross campus, and the high school Camden campus. In addition, our lease with the Campbell Union High School District was terminating in June 1987. Added to all of these challenges, salaries remained less than half those paid by the local public schools. VCS was fighting a losing battle to attract quality teachers while academic standards persistently declined.

Get to Know the "Boss"

Devote yourself to knowing God at increasingly deeper levels. The more you get to know His nature, character and works, the more He will accomplish His supernatural work through you—naturally

Stay Tuned and Keep Talking

Pray regularly as a spiritual discipline. Give God your full attention so He has opportunity to speak to you about anything, including matters that are not already on your mind. As you develop a God-consciousness in all you do, you will find it easier to keep your ear tuned to God's Spirit and maintain a dialog with Him throughout the day. Listen for God to speak into your thoughts in every situation. Even if the answer seems obvious, do not ignore the possibility that He may have something to say, if only to confirm your thoughts. He may surprise you.

Chapter 22: 1, 3

Again I poured out my heart to the Lord about the futility of captaining a ship on its way down. This time I sensed a strong response: "I, not you, am Captain of this ship. It's not going down with Me on board. I'm going to turn this ship around." My eyes widened as my faith rose. It would take a miracle. But I remembered the Gospel stories about the disciples sailing on the Sea of Galilee. When Jesus is on board, I realized, the ship never sinks, no matter how fierce the storm.

Although we wanted to purchase the high school campus we were leasing, a developer planned to build a shopping center and custom homes on the land. He paid the school district a price per acre completely out of our range. After many months wondering whether our high school students would have a home the next fall, VCS negotiated a one-year lease extension with him by April 1, 1987, giving us some breathing room.

In May the high school principal resigned and I took on that additional role, moving my offices to the Camden High School campus. I had serious concerns about the atmosphere that pervaded the campus. During its former season of accelerated enrollment, VCS had adopted strict rules for dress, behavior, and lifestyle in an effort to "keep the high school Christian." Intended to maintain strong Christian standards, the regulations instead often blurred the distinction between biblical principles and institutional standards. Many rules were justified with scriptural quotations often unintentionally taken out of context. Boys had to keep their hair cut short. Girls could not wear pants. Cheerleaders were not permitted to combine movement and music lest they cross the line into "sinful" dance. All forms of affection between boys and girls, including handholding, met with immediate disapproval.

The standards—and their swift and harsh enforce-
ment—rankled many. Students often called the high school
"Valley Christian Prison." Some parents of local public
school students threatened to send their children to Valley
Christian High if they got out of line. One VCS parent
warned his son, "If attending Valley doesn't improve your
behavior, I'll transfer you to a military boarding school."

This legalistic approach proved disastrous. The
rule-oriented perspective misrepresented biblical Christian faith. When students disagreed with the school's standards, they often thought they were rejecting God as well,
because they mistakenly understood the school's rules to
have come from God.

Such a poisoned atmosphere contributed to the
enrollment decline, the struggle to hire good teachers, and
poor relations between faculty and students. Despite the
reassurance of Captain Jesus, I wondered, *How can this
ship be saved?*

**Maintain an Integrated Christ-Centered
Focus on Excellence in All   Academic and
Co-curricular Programs**
    Develop a school culture of "grace and
truth" (John 1:14).

Chapter 18: 1- D- 2

FROM RULES TO RELATIONSHIP

I sensed God's mandate for me during the 1987–88
school year in my newly added role as high school principal was to transform this "rules" orientation to a "relationship" orientation centered around grace. I heard the divine
message loud and clear: "If you expel legalism from this

school, I will bless the school beyond anything you can imagine." With the support of the VCS board of directors, I rewrote the *Student/Parent Handbook* in an effort to distinguish principles from preferences and to avoid confusing human institutional standards with biblical Christian standards. In the process we hoped to develop a school culture of "grace and truth" (John 1:14). The regulation on boys' haircuts was relaxed. Girls' pants became an acceptable part of the school dress code. The rule against any "public display of affection" (PDA) became a rule against inappropriate PDA.

The changes showed up all over campus and beyond. Cheerleaders added music to their routines and learned to evaluate its appropriateness. Parents, not the school, were expected to decide whether private parties should include dance. The band director was given permission to play "Rock Around the Clock."

Most important, students began to reflect more seriously on their relationship with our Lord Jesus rather than on just the school rules. The new approach sought to foster a loving, Christ-centered atmosphere that attracted rather than coerced students toward faith. I discovered many wonderful teachers who were praying for such changes, who wanted the school's leadership to reflect the fruit of the Spirit as Christian role models.

With the understanding that profound doubt often precedes mature faith, we began to encourage more discussion, debate, and analysis. Our goal became internalization of faith rather than a "lecture, learn, and test" method. Students were challenged to reflect on what they should believe and why, thoughtfully considering the teachings of Jesus Christ before making a commitment to follow Him as Lord and Savior. With this approach, we no longer required students to express their Christian faith as a requirement for admission. Instead, students agreed to give the claims and teachings of Jesus Christ a fair hearing.

Eventually our students discovered it is a privilege to attend Valley Christian High School. I wanted all high school students to make a personal decision to attend, so I announced this offer: "I'll help you transfer to another high school of your choice if you are not happy with VCHS." Qualified freshmen that preferred to attend another school with their friends could be admitted to Valley at their parents' request with an agreement to transfer out by the end of the first semester if the student did not choose to remain. Very few students left.

Maintain an Integrated Christ-Centered Focus on Excellence in All Academic and Co-curricular Programs
Allow students to internalize Christian faith through personal choice, rather than using an indoctrination approach to inculcate religious instruction.

Chapter 18: 1-D-5

Many parents, teachers, staff, administrators, and board members wholeheartedly joined the efforts to restore a nurturing atmosphere of God's love. While rules and high standards must remain part of every quality school, only concerted efforts to differentiate biblical principles from institutional preferences will keep legalism in check. The challenge continues to this day.

OH, GIVE ME A HOME . . .

With the new orientation at VCS, a welcome breeze of God's goodness began clearing the air. But the critical predicament concerning the high school's site continued to loom just around the corner. Entering May 1988, we didn't know where Valley would be able to offer high school education in September. At nearly the eleventh hour, the Lord provided another one-year lease extension from the developer who had bought the Camden campus. But to those who didn't sense God's assurance, it appeared that our efforts merely held potential disaster at bay. The school still faced the possibility of closure by June 1989 if another campus did not become available.

Confronted with such uncertainty, many parents lost confidence about the future stability of VCS facilities. Enrollment continued to drop, reducing tuition income and squeezing our staff even further. *If only we had a permanent home campus. . . .* How I yearned for a place to call our own. We floated a number of ideas for building or acquiring property, but none went anywhere. The school's changes over the past year were heartening, but would mean little if Valley went under. Clinging to God's promises became the antidote to fears that had overwhelmed me when I initially dismissed the superintendent's job with the observation that "VCS doesn't have enough life boats!"

CHAPTER 2
VALLEY ON A HILL?

I set down my coffee mug and I began to pace my office. Valley's facility crisis pressed on my consciousness relentlessly. By June 1988, only a few months away, our high school students would have just one last year at the Camden campus before becoming homeless. How could the school, the students, or their parents make any long-range plans with this kind of uncertainty?

Valley Christian Schools had recently given up on one of its previous ideas for acquiring its own facilities. Twelve acres of land that proved unsuitable for developing a school were sold for $4.2 million, closing the door on this option but providing VCS with liquid assets. These funds enabled us to deal with our backbreaking financial arrears. Our debt totaled just over $1 million, while the annual budget at that time was only a bit more than $3 million. (On top of the $420,000 deficit my first year, we had borrowed $600,000 to cover past shortfalls.) After the sale of these twelve acres, we paid all current debts and were able to sock away about $3 million toward the dream of our own future campus—a small down payment, but enough to stir glimmers of hope.

My thoughts returned to the offer that had surfaced out of the blue the year before. The tantalizing opportunity, at first so thrilling, now seemed to tease us from just beyond our reach. Betty Roeder, owner of the Great Oaks Water Company, was impressed by positive reports about Valley Christian from the high school son of one of her key employees. She had heard about the looming lease termination at the Camden campus and the board's persistent but futile efforts to locate land or facilities where VCS could lease or build another campus.

Mrs. Roeder owned twenty-five acres of property near the intersection of Skyway Drive and Monterey Highway in San Jose. I remembered our astonishment when she offered the land to us for only $1.00 per square foot (about $43,500 per acre)—an incredibly generous offer, when other Silicon Valley property had recently sold as high as $23.00 per square foot for residential construction.

My first trip to inspect her land took me up a hill where I admired a magnificent 360-degree view of the surrounding city. The property, however, included steep slopes that would complicate development. With great reluctance, we eventually judged the acreage insufficient and unsuitable for the needed facilities and athletic fields to construct a comprehensive high school.

Yet my mind would not let the issue rest. *"Who owns the adjacent hill property?"* I wondered. We learned that an additional thirty-two acres belonged to a local developer. He had no desire to sell, however. In fact, he told us that he and Betty Roeder had planned a joint venture to build several hundred homes on the hill. Mrs. Roeder acknowledged the one-time plan but said she had dissolved her partnership with him. She wanted VCS to have the land—but even at her bargain-offering price, the acreage would never work for a high school campus.

My coffee grew cold as I stared out my office window. Over the past weeks others and I had prayed about this situation, asking the Holy Spirit to move the developer to release his property for purchase. Without Betty Roeder's property, the joint residential development they had planned would not be able to proceed. Nevertheless he held his ground.

Something kept nudging me to pursue Betty's offer, however—something I recognized as the prompting of the Spirit of God. I had this crazy notion that if we moved forward with arrangements to purchase the Roeder property, God would supernaturally persuade the other owner to sell his land. With growing conviction, I stepped back to my desk and picked up the phone.

CREATIVE NEGOTIATIONS

Betty Roeder was delighted to renew dialog with us about the sale of her hill property. But there was another complication. I learned that a local church had earlier approached Betty Roeder about selling or donating her land for construction of a new church.

The church heard about our discussions and assumed the school was cutting in on its negotiations. When I learned of the church's earlier approaches to Betty Roeder and their concerns, I talked with the church's pastor and assured him that VCS would not compete with the church for purchase of the hill property. Rather than bidding against each other, I suggested, we should seek the Lord's will. "If God wants the property for a church," I told him, "the school will not interfere."

Betty Roeder continued to assure us of her preference to make her land available for building a school, although she was not opposed to a church. I mulled over the situation, still sensing the Lord's prompting to proceed despite no sign of movement on the developer's part.

During my prayerful pondering, a strong passion and plan came to mind, and I made an appointment with the pastor. After I greeted his secretary, she took me to meet him in his nicely appointed office, where I laid out my proposal. If we could acquire the developer's property, VCS would loan the church the funds to buy approximately eleven of the acres on which to build their new church. Costs for putting in roads, parking lots, and other infrastructure would be apportioned according to the terms of a joint development agreement. I rolled out a plot plan of the site and suggested that we could build both a church and a school, sharing expenses and parking spaces.

The minister was intrigued. Within a few days I heard back from him. He was ready to move forward with the idea. My heart leaped! I couldn't wait to inform our VCS board of directors. Seeking assurance, I asked Bob Wallace, a VCS board member, to walk the property with me. While overlooking the San Jose skyline, Bob had three words: "Tie it up."

This proposal met with everyone's approval— everyone except the developer's, that is. Sensing God's strong assurance, I then approached the other owner again.

We met in his office, where the tanned and athletic deal-maker had photos showing him engaged in his hobby of race walking.

"Betty Roeder has agreed to sell her property to Valley Christian Schools," I told him. "Without her land for your joint residential development, it seems to make sense for you to sell your property to the school as well."

We discussed the idea. He seemed willing to nego- tiate, but insisted on receiving market value for his land.

I swallowed as I sensed what I thought might be a God-given reply. "Well," I began, "market value, as you know, is determined by the most recent sale of similar nearby property. Valley Christian just purchased Betty Roeder's adjacent land on the hill for $1.00 per square foot."

The developer stared for a moment in stunned silence. He insisted that he needed considerably more for his property. Further, he said he wanted to retain several of his thirty-two acres to construct town homes.

As we continued our conversation, I asked the Lord to give me wisdom and favor. A notion began to take shape, and I made a suggestion: "What if you agree to a purchase price of $1.00 per square foot and donate to the school your estimate of the remaining value of your property as a charitable contribution and a tax write-off?"

TWISTS AND TURNS

The developer needed some time to consider the idea. After consulting with his accountants, he contacted me. I nearly burst with joy when he agreed to our suggested terms. He insisted, however, on holding back nine acres on the northeast side of the hill for development of town homes. This land included the four-acre area known as the "terraces" and five more acres on the east side of Diamond Heights Drive, the only access road to the land at that time. He said that before we could finalize the deal for his remaining twenty-three acres we would have to obtain a lot-line adjustment from the City of San Jose to separate the land he wanted to retain. Although the road would have provided a clear boundary, the terraces adjoined the rest of the hill property and could not be separated without a lot-line adjustment.

"OK, if that's what we need, let's get it!" I was ready to barrel ahead at full speed. Then a response from the City of San Jose threw on the brakes: *Not so fast*. Before city planners could make a lot-line adjustment, we needed to submit a development plan for their approval. And they couldn't authorize any such plan without an Environmental Impact Report (EIR) and other legal requirements.

Well, how much time and money will that take? I wondered. Plenty, as it turned out. The serpentine rock on the hill property contained asbestos. Earthmoving could release dangerous airborne fibers of this mineral, so no one would even consider letting us build without a lengthy and costly EIR.

The school couldn't afford to put such time and resources into an EIR process before even acquiring title. Yet we couldn't acquire title without the EIR and lot-line adjustment. As long as the developer insisted on holding back the terraces, the entire project seemed dead.

I couldn't believe God would bring us so close to purchasing this property for no purpose. *"Lord, what's Your solution here?"*

Soon another crazy notion began to materialize. What if the school bought the twenty-three acres he was offering us but received title to his entire property west of Diamond Heights Drive, including the terraces? We would work out a separate agreement for the school to "sell back" to him the four-acre terraces, for a nominal $1.00, as soon as the City of San Jose approved a development plan for either the school's first building or the development of town homes, whichever came first. We would avoid a costly process to obtain the lot-line adjustment, and he would retain title to his five acres on the east side of the road.

I took this idea to the developer, and he gave it the nod. VCS completed the $2.1 million purchase of both the Roeder and his hill properties in February 1989. With the deal in hand, the school negotiated with South Valley Christian Church on terms of our joint purchase, joint development, and joint maintenance agreements. The church later reimbursed VCS, at $1.00 per square foot, the price for the acreage on which it planned to build its new facility.

Only the providential hand of God could have guided these complex and innovative transactions. The church got the property it wanted, the developer retained five of the nine acres he wanted along with the right to buy back the other four acres for one dollar, and the school got title to the property without a special lot-line adjustment. With exhilaration, we prepared to move forward with our school building plans.

FULL SPEED AHEAD—OR
DEAD IN THE WATER?

I was so charged up about this awesome chain of events that I expected smooth sailing from here on. I knew fundraising for construction would present a challenge because donors felt stressed by our all-too-frequent crisis appeals to cover the annual budget deficits. But with the conviction that the school belonged to the Lord and that anything is possible with God, VCS launched a three-year capital campaign called "Build the Dream and Experience the Vision."

We hired a consultant to prepare the Environmental Impact Report. David Powers and his team from Powers and Associates began to work out a plan to mitigate the risks associated with airborne asbestos fibers so we could proceed with grading and construction.

Hopes ran high that Valley Christian Schools could build a new campus on the hill for both the junior and senior high schools within two years after close of escrow. We would still have to find a temporary location for the senior high when it was bumped from the Camden campus in June 1989, but we trusted that God would provide.

Then a shocking report came from Gerry DeYoung, a principal with Ruth and Going, Inc., an architectural, engineering, and planning firm that VCS had hired. We were waiting in suspense while biologists investigated whether our land provided habitat for the rare, endangered, and protected Bay Checkerspot butterfly (*Euphydryas editha bayensis*). All development plans like ours had to be cleared of any risk to this species, found only in the San Francisco Bay region.

"I have some good news and some bad news for you," Gerry DeYoung reported to our joint school and church building committee. "First, the good news. There is no habitat for the Bay Checkerspot butterfly on the hill. That's the good news—but now for the bad news. Although the biologists didn't find a habitat for the butter-flies, they were thrilled to make the unexpected discovery of rare and endangered plants growing on the hill." His voice resonated with obvious dismay.

I was afraid to ask: "What exactly does that mean for our building plans?"

Gerry explained that no construction could occur that would destroy any habitat occupied by the Metcalf Canyon Jewelflower or the Dudleya flowering plant, both legally protected. The penalties involved serious jail time.

I shook my head in disbelief. How many roadblocks could one project face? This discovery put everything at risk. The school's fledgling capital campaign, after raising almost $300,000, ground to a halt.

"Lord, You know how much we need our own campus," I lamented. "I thought You were guiding us to purchase and develop this property. In fact, I still think we followed Your leading and You've worked wonders to bring us to this point. So what's going on?"

Closing my eyes, I imagined the weeds growing on the hill—our hill, now—with the panoramic view. "You made these plants, Lord, and I like plants as much as any-one. But what are You going to do about them?"

The answers would be a long time in coming.

CHAPTER 3
A SCHOOL WITHOUT A HOME

I'm not sure when I looked forward to a vacation so much. After the devastating news about the endangered plants on our hill property, Valley Christian Schools still needed to find a site for the high school in time for the start of the 1989–90 academic school year. For two years, during our lease extensions on the Camden campus, the administrative leadership team had turned over every possible stone in our search for another location. Now the developer was finally evicting our students from Camden, and no adequate facilities had come to light anywhere in the South Bay's Silicon Valley.

In spring of 1989, with no other options, we reluctantly signed a lease with the Union School District in San Jose on a small, former elementary school. The Vineland campus, now vacant, adjoined a fifty-acre site we hoped to purchase. A clause in our contract stated that if anyone should offer the school district cash without contingencies to purchase the property, we would lose our lease immediately. The clause made me uncomfortable, yet VCS had no choice but to accept these terms if we hoped to open the high school that fall. Besides, such an offer, coming out of the blue, seemed unlikely.

After the spring semester ended, we moved Valley Christian High School out of the Camden campus and into the Vineland Elementary campus in preparation for the start of school on Tuesday, September 5. We shoehorned everything we could into the small, inadequate facilities, temporarily grateful the high school enrollment had shrunk to 263 students. When all at last seemed ready, Kris and I left on a three-week vacation with our Silver

Streak trailer. I felt as though we had just staggered off the front lines of a battle zone after a hard-won victory — bushed, but still breathing.

On our way back after touring national parks, Kris and I stopped to visit my brother Gene and his wife, Kathy. We enjoyed staying at their rural home near Atwater, California, 120 miles east of San Jose. Kris and Kathy are identical twin sisters, and we had a great family time together.

On our last full day of vacation, I was sitting at their kitchen table when the telephone rang. Kathy handed the phone to me. The caller was Steve Vaughn, VCS Director of Publications. I couldn't figure out how he had obtained my brother's phone number, but I didn't have an opportunity to ask.

"I know you're still on vacation," Steve said, "and I hate to be the one to bring bad news, but you need to know: We don't have a campus for the high school." The improbable — the unthinkable — had happened. Dividend Development Corporation had offered Union School District a no-contingency cash offer of $1 million per acre for the Vineland campus and the adjacent fifty acres, immediately displacing Valley Christian. With little more than two weeks before the first day of the fall semester, our high school had no home.

Steve filled me in as I processed this stunning news. My pulse began to race and my arms and legs felt weak and shaky. Yet along with the shock I also felt a rush of faith and the assurance that God was bigger than this problem.

"Well, Steve," I said finally, "we are now going to discover just how powerful God is and how much He cares for VCS. This is an impossible situation except for God's miraculous provision — so there's a big miracle on the way."

I told Steve I would be home the next day and in the office on Monday morning. As I hung up the phone I recognized with gratitude that God had held back this news long enough for Kris and me to enjoy our vacation.

BETWEEN PHARAOH AND THE RED SEA

During our drive back to San Jose, the reality of the situation kept settling in, almost like dealing with the sudden death of a loved one. My emotions seesawed between fear and faith. On the one hand I sensed a great peace and comfort from the Lord. *If God is able to resurrect the dead, He is able to raise up Valley Christian High School before the fall semester starts in two weeks,* I affirmed. Then anxiety surged as I reflected on how we had spent the past two years searching for alternate sites to no avail.

Worn out from the pendulum swings, I finally took charge of my racing thoughts. *Emotions aren't going to control this situation,* I declared silently. *God is in control regardless of my fears.*

On Monday morning, August 21, the VCS administrative leadership team gathered in a classroom at the Vineland campus to face this crisis head-on. We had already considered and eliminated every other possible site in the Silicon Valley, but once again we listed each location on the blackboard. Once again we noted pros and cons. Once again we drew a chalk line through every location on the list. Every site seemed impossible to use. All circumstances indicated that Valley Christian High School would not open in September.

Administrators slumped in discouragement. "There's no answer," one stated, as others shook their heads. "Nothing is available."

In contrast, I felt a growing excitement. We faced

an impossible situation with no alternatives, like the children of Israel fleeing Egypt, blocked by the Red Sea with
Pharaoh's army in hot pursuit. Yet as we prayed together,
I had a strong inner assurance that God did not want
the school to close. With all human options eliminated,
God now had opportunity to demonstrate that He alone
is Founder, Provider, and Sustainer of Valley Christian
Schools. This circumstance called for a miracle—and I
was eager to see how God would pull it off.

    We left the meeting with a mixture of faith and help-
less dependence on God. In the parking lot afterwards, I
ran into Al Kosters, principal of San Jose Christian School
and parent of a VCS high school student. He suggested
that I take another look at one of the sites we had crossed
off our long blackboard list. Campbell Community Center
was the former site of Campbell High School. The City of
Campbell had purchased the campus and converted it into
the Campbell Community Center. Our previous inquiries
revealed that only six classrooms were available for lease,
far fewer than we needed. Linda Roberts, the center's
director, had seemed sympathetic to Valley's plight but
explained that various groups regularly used the athletic
fields, gyms, weight room, and band room.

    I reminded Al of these obstacles we had already
encountered. Yet, inexplicably, I felt a powerful tug in my
spirit that God was speaking through Al about revisiting
the possibility of using Campbell Community Center for
our high school. When I returned to the office I immediately called to set up another appointment with Linda
Roberts.

    As I drove to the center later that same day, I sensed
the warm presence of the Holy Spirit and a deep, unrea-
sonable assurance that all was well. I didn't know exactly
what God would do, but I felt confident He was unfolding

His wonderful master plan. I simply needed to follow His lead.

THE IMPOSSIBLE TAKES SHAPE

When I arrived at Linda Roberts' office, she greeted me warmly, but facts had not changed. "We still have only six classrooms available for lease," she confirmed.

We talked a bit, and I asked for another tour of the site. As we walked across the grounds, I prayed silently, my spirit and senses alert. *God has a plan to make this campus our home,* I thought.

I noticed some open space between the classrooms and the softball field, and a picture began to form in my mind. "Linda, would the city allow VCS to install modular buildings in this area?"

"Well, that's an idea," she replied with a thoughtful look. "But you'd need a special action by the City Council members to approve it, and they're on vacation now."

A grimace crossed my face. But I continued praying, and despite the impossibly short timeline, I felt the Holy Spirit urging me, *Go for it!*

Linda and I continued walking the grounds, passing the gyms, the band room, and the athletic fields. She reiterated that these facilities could not be leased because community groups used them.

"Hmm." My eyes squinted slightly as another idea took shape. "When exactly do these groups come? Is there a possibility we could coordinate schedules and rent the space on an hourly basis?"

Linda stopped a moment. "Let's take a look at the schedule," she said.

Back in her office, we discovered that the community groups did not use those facilities until about 4:30 or 5:00 in the evening. Valley Christian High School could rent after school and still accommodate athletic practices by other groups after 5:00. Moreover, a food service program was available that could provide lunch meals for students. With careful scheduling we worked out a hypothetical plan that would provide about $300,000 of additional annual revenue to the city and a beautiful home for VCHS.

I could hardly contain my excitement. This situation was so much better than the elementary campus we had lost. Linda agreed, but pulled me back to reality. "Great plan, but the big problem is timing. School starts in two weeks, and the city bureaucracy just doesn't move that fast, especially during August with the council members on vacation in various parts of the globe."

Her words spoke sobering truth, but the flow of elation now carried me irresistibly in its grip. "I think we have no choice but to try to contact them," I replied. Linda agreed to make the effort through the city manager's office.

CLAMBERING TO SECURE
THE FOUNDATIONS

Within a couple of days, Linda and I talked again. "It's amazing!" she said. "I've never seen such fast action in the city. Every one of the council members was contacted and agreed with the plan by phone. We even reached the member traveling in Brazil." Her astonishment spilled out in a couple of comments hinting that this turn of events seemed miraculous.

Empowered with the city's approval, Valley began a furious search for modular buildings. One would become the high school offices, and two more provided three classrooms each. I realized we would need additional time to move, and postponed the opening of school six days until Monday, September 11. We barely had time to get the word out to parents about our new location and the new start date.

Over Labor Day weekend a volunteer army of parents, students, and staff helped move the school using ten tractor-trailers. Teachers began setting up classrooms that week. Although we were still assembling the modular buildings, God worked His wonders and the high school opened on September 11. During the six weeks of construction, Pastor Mike Kiley at The Home Church next door provided temporary classrooms for our students.

As the 1989–90 school year started, the atmosphere on our campuses seemed more positive and full of hope than at any time since I had become superintendent. Everyone appreciated the fresh focus on grace instead of legalism. The spiritual tone of VCS improved dramatically.

As a relatively new superintendent, I made a point of trying to listen to the school family members about their concerns and perspectives. We initiated surveys of both students and parents to learn how effectively they thought the superintendent, administration, faculty, and staffs were serving them. We pinpointed areas where the educational quality at VCS could improve.

I still faced many painful decisions, including unavoidable budget cuts as well as faculty and staff changes needed for the sake of the ministry. Many days and nights I wrestled with situations, seeking the Lord's guidance. The VCS board of directors, thankfully, provided crucial wisdom and encouragement during this season of difficult but necessary choices. Without the Lord's help through their support, direction, and Spirit-inspired leadership, the school would have failed.

By the summer of 1990 some of these decisions began bearing fruit with an improved quality of education. Confidence rose in the stability of our campus facilities, and years of slumping enrollment reversed.

We had turned a corner, but many questions remained. *Can this growth be sustained?* I wondered. We still faced frustrating budget deficits and inadequate salaries. Low enrollment and insufficient tuition did not meet expenses. *But suppose VCS does continue to grow—our students will split the seams at the Campbell Community Center! Then where will we go?*

The property on the hill still danced in my dreams. After scrambling to secure rented campuses not once but twice within a year, I longed for the security of owning our own school home. But the endangered plants still presented an apparently insurmountable obstacle to construction. Initial estimates to conduct a three-year pilot study to move the plants ranged from $200,000 to $300,000 with no assurance of a resolution. Painfully we concluded we could not afford the pilot studies with the prospect of success so slim. The vision of building on our hill loomed well beyond reach, like a mountaintop obscured by a storm.

CHAPTER 4

THE POWER OF SACRIFICE

"Kris, would you like to go for a ride?"

It was a sunny summer day and the great outdoors beckoned. My wife had the day off from her work as a teacher at Neighborhood Christian Preschool in Santa Clara. "I'd like to show you the property VCS purchased last year," I explained.

Kris was happy to go. We headed off in our brown 1985 Nissan Sentra. The only road leading to the hill, Diamond Heights Drive, approached from the northeast and led to a ramshackle house and barn, the only buildings we owned. Valley Christian Schools rented the home in "as is" condition to a young man at a low rate in exchange for him keeping an eye on the property.

I parked the car, and Kris and I got out to walk. Summer sun had turned most of the open scrubland the color of straw.

The fresh air and sky helped to clear the thoughts cluttering my brain. *What a shame,* I mused. *This beautiful and valuable property belongs to Valley, but we can't use it for a school.* Elsewhere on our acreage the endangered wildflowers waved their stems with impunity, unaware of the legal protection that granted them the clout to hold back bulldozers.

Once again the commanding vista at the top of the hill seized my attention. Kris and I stood quietly, turning our view in each direction. *What do You want for this property, Lord?* I wondered. *Is it time to abandon the idea of building a school here? Was it Your purpose for us to buy this land as an investment to sell so we could use the profits for another campus?*

We walked a short distance, following the ridge-line, when suddenly Kris called out, "Look—what's that?" A huddled, furry mass rose above the grass near our path, and we approached warily to investigate. What we found sickened us. The headless body of a German shepherd dog lay on the slope.

Kris and I stared at the dead dog, and I spoke aloud what we both knew: "Beheadings don't happen by accident." Because of the body's location on a hilltop, I suspected that the animal was slaughtered as part of some occult ritual sacrifice.

Righteous anger rose in my spirit. "This property belongs to God!" I declared. "Whoever did this is trespassing—legally and spiritually!" Kris and I continued to walk the hill, and I silently proclaimed God's ownership and intention to accomplish His purposes there.

On our way back, we stopped at the old home on the property and knocked on the door. After a moment, Chris, the young man renting the house, appeared. He was surprised to have visitors in this isolated location, until he recognized his landlord.

I explained what Kris and I had just found. "Do you know anything about how this happened?" I asked.

Chris nodded. "Yeah, they come up here and start chanting from time to time," he said. "It's pretty common. I wasn't aware of the dog, but I'm not surprised."

His experience confirmed my suspicions. Occult groups, I knew, often use high places to conduct blood sacrifices with the hope of harnessing and wielding spiritual power.

As Kris and I drove home, it dawned on me more clearly than ever that Valley Christian Schools was engaged in a spiritual battle. Not all the obstacles to building our campus on the hill property rose from mere human or natural difficulties. The forces of evil evidently wanted to claim this ground, too.

My swirling thoughts came to rest on one center point: *Well, the blood sacrifice of Christ on the cross trumps the power of all other sacrifices.* In my spirit I resolved with rock-solid conviction: *If the devil thinks he can thwart God's plans, he's in for a fight with this property's owner, Jesus!*

WHY NOT THE BEST?

With building plans stalled, we turned our focus toward continued school improvement. We had already begun seeing the fruit of the fresh orientation toward grace rather than rules. As the 1990–91 school year started that fall, I introduced a new emphasis at VCS.

Maintain an Integrated Christ-Centered Focus on Excellence in All Academic and Co-curricular Programs.

Develop a school culture of "grace and truth" (John 1:14).

Chapter 18:1-D-2

The Lord was speaking to me about His desire that Valley Christian Schools reflect His excellence. I had read *In Search of Excellence: Lessons from America's Best-Run Companies* by Thomas J. Peters and Robert H. Waterman, Jr. Their book prompted serious contemplation about the nature of excellence, and the Holy Spirit began connecting some dots for me.

For several years I had wrestled with the realization that many people, Christians included perceived Christian schools as often substandard and second-rate. Why did Christian schools, businesses, books, and movies all too frequently convey an image of mediocrity to the world's arbiters of quality? Why did God's people have to settle for less than the best when making choices they hoped would respect His values? I cringed at how often a God-honoring alternative to secular culture was dismissed as a joke.

We believers, I realized, tend to see ourselves as underdogs in a social order set against biblical principles. We often think that a poor financial position and consequent inferior quality is the price we must pay for maintaining Christian values. As long as we're "doing our best" in such difficult circumstances, it's easy to rationalize that our efforts are worthy as a "spiritual sacrifice" even when they fall short of what non-Christians are producing.

I began sharing my thoughts with everyone who would listen, from the board and administrators to faculty, parents, and many others. "God has provided all the resources we need to represent Him faithfully and reflect His glory," I said. "Why shouldn't Christians have the top schools, the finest art and literature, the highest quality people producing the best in every field? God's resources are unlimited!"

This redirection of focus quietly took on a life of its own. I started calling the emphasis the "Quest for Excellence™." The key to the success of the Quest for Excellence is in the definition of "excellence." We began to understand that the definition of "excellence" at Valley Christian Schools involves the nature, character, and works of God. The word "quest" communicates the idea that we are on a journey toward God's excellence and that we cannot reach our destination this side of heaven. According to 1 John 3:2, " . . . when He is revealed, we shall be like Him."

The new initiative rested on a bold but sensible philosophic foundation: By shifting the focus of our efforts from survival to the "Quest for Excellence™," God's purposes would naturally follow. By pouring resources into adding and upgrading programs and then showcasing those programs through improved publications and public relations efforts, the school would attract new students. The added revenue from increased enrollment could then be reinvested into more program improvements. These enhancements, including better faculty salaries, would in turn draw applications from better teachers, further boosting educational quality as well as demand for admissions.

In the process, VCS aimed for less school-centeredness with more responsive care for parents. I have always affirmed that parents are the primary educators of their children under God. This theme took on new significance as we emphasized that the school existed to serve God by serving parents as their children's primary educators, and that VCS best serves parents by providing an excellent formal education to their children.

Parents: Are the primary educators of their children under God.

School Leaders and Teachers: Help students discover their unique God-given talents through comprehensive innovative programs

Chapter 20: 1 & 4

RISKING DOUBLE OR NOTHING

As I saw it, the Quest for Excellence emphasis posed the only hope for the school's financial success. VCS still faced overwhelming annual budget deficits. In the past, our crisis fundraising efforts—"help us or we die"—left donors with a distasteful sense of being manipulated for their dollars. Many people gave with the attitude, "All right, I'll bail you out this time (again), but would you please get your financial house in order and run the school with the same good business practices that all successful businesses follow?"

Contributions based on guilt and the threat of disaster brought no joy to the givers. In contrast, I was convinced that if donors got excited about a specific program or about special educational enhancements, they would give joyfully from the heart.

I asked administrators and department heads to dream about what kind of programs they would like to see offered and to pray that God would give them "the desires of their hearts." The idea, based on Psalm 37:4, was that God puts His own desires into our hearts so that He can achieve His ambitions through us as we delight in Him. Then we can "brag on what God is doing" when these desires are realized. I encouraged department heads to stretch their faith to imagine educational offerings so excellent and unique that people would say, "If you want that, you have to go to Valley Christian."

> **The test for every department is when people say, "If you want that (a distinctive program or quality), you must go to (Your School Name) Christian School."**
>
> Chapter 18: 5-E
>
> **Aim For The Stars**
> Aim for excellence in everything you do. Understand that, ultimately, true excellence is the nature, character, and works of God. Anything we do that truly reflects excellence requires the work of God and is by definition "supernatural." Pursuing His excellence opens the door to experiencing His supernatural activity in your everyday life—naturally.
>
> Chapter 22: 19

Despite the substantial added expense this change of emphasis would initially require, an unshakable conviction grew that this was God's direction for Valley Christian Schools. Gradually, I came to understand that the school's success rested on the success of the Quest for Excellence™. I reasoned that the Quest for Excellence would help VCS more accurately reflect the nature, character, and works of God and put the school on a solid financial foundation. Moreover, the focus on building a school of extraordinary quality would attract people of means to enroll their children and help develop the school's programs.

I was blessed to have the unswerving support of the VCS board, including Dr. Rick Watson, who became board chair in 1991. Rick's ongoing passion for the "Quest" challenged me and the board to accomplish all that God intended. Despite our existing deficits, we determined to seek every opportunity to improve our curriculum, facilities, programs, faculty, publications, and public relations.

Maintain an Integrated Christ-Centered Focus on Excellence in All Academic and Co-curricular Programs

Inform students that God is preparing them to restore respect for Christian faith in the marketplace of ideas, with the goal of fulfilling Christ's commission to "Go to the people of all nations and make them my disciples" through their personal Quests for Excellence (Matthew 28:19a, CEV).

Chapter 18: 1-A

Measure, Monitor, and Manage All Elements of Quality to Put the Organization on a Solid Management and Business Foundation

"Not slothful in business; fervent in spirit; serving the Lord" (Romans 12:11, KJV)

Chapter 19: 5

EXCELLENCE BRINGS INFLUENCE™

The pursuit of excellence motivated me because I began to understand that Excellence Brings Influence™. I realized the most excellent professionals and institutions command the most powerful spheres of influence for shaping the future of America's cultural conscience involving what is right and wrong. The question becomes, "Will Christian professionals be among the most excellent influencers that shape the moral values of our culture?" I became convinced that Valley Christian Schools must reject the mistaken emphasis of the past century that "separation from the world is holiness unto God." In short, we must stop sheltering our students from the world and prepare them to invade and transform our culture with the Truth. We must challenge our students to serve Christ by becoming the most excellent Christian professionals of influence in the world.

I became convinced that God is equipping an army of Christian school students with the knowledge of God's Word and a passionate commitment to transform society through their emerging professions of influence. This "Excellence Brings Influence" movement in Christian schools is nothing less than a work of God to bring an old-fashioned revival to the 21st century. The mighty influence of the pulpit and the tent meetings of past revivals that brought Christian faith to our nation is now moving into the professions that shape our culture, including the arts, educational, entertainment, financial, legal, legislative, media, and other spheres. These professions of influence powerfully shape the moral and cultural values of our nation and much of the world.

I understood that the Christian school movement involves a plan of God to reintroduce Christian faith to our culture. But to be effective, comprehensive Christian schools must become so excellent that they are unrivaled or at least among the finest schools in their communities. Christian schools must emerge as the best schools that prepare the most qualified students to enter the most preeminent universities if we are to produce the most excellent professionals who will influence and reshape the spiritual and moral values of the 21st century.

The Bible is full of people God used to implement this strategy. Daniel and the three other Hebrew youth were promoted to serve King Nebuchadnezzar because they had "intelligence in every branch of wisdom, endowed with understanding and discerning knowledge"

(Daniel 1:4, NAS). These godly young men became the most influential professionals in Babylon because Excellence Brings Influence™. They transformed their culture and brought a respect for the Most High God in an otherwise godless nation. King Nebuchadnezzar and King Darius made decrees that honored the Most High God before the entire nation because the excellence of Daniel and his three Hebrew companions brought influence that they used for God's glory (see Daniel 3:28–4:37 and 6:25–28).

Daniel's redemptive influence was rooted in his excellent spirit, knowledge, and wisdom. "Then this Daniel was preferred above the presidents and princes, because an excellent spirit was in him" (Daniel 6:3, KJV). King Belshazzar said to Daniel, "I have heard of you, that the Spirit of God is in you, and that light and understanding and excellent wisdom are found in you" (Daniel 5:14). God's strategy of challenging, educating, transforming, and commissioning young people to reflect God's excellence in order to restore respect to the Most High God among godless nations was clearly effective. His Excellence Brings Influence strategic plan will fill the emerging "pulpits" among the professions of influence during the 21st century.

Similar examples show how God promoted people of excellence to positions of professional influence to engage and spiritually transform their culture. These leaders include Abraham, Moses, Boaz, David, Nehemiah, the patriarch Joseph, Esther, Mary (a domestic engineer), and her husband Joseph (a carpenter and the CEO of his family). While the professions of these Bible characters vary widely, all are people through whom God worked greatly to achieve a powerful redemptive influence in the world.

They each had a passion to reflect the nature, character, and works of God. People who pursue God's nature and character make themselves candidates to serve as conduits for the works of God.

VISION FROM THE EDGE OF THE ABYSS

Explaining this insight brought sympathetic nods, but many people at VCS had serious jitters about committing the needed funds to launch and improve programs in the face of scarce resources. It helped that Valley's enrollment had begun an upswing after we secured the Campbell campus facilities for the high school. Still, we would need many more students, tuition increases, financial contributions, a great deal of faith, and patience. During this crucial time VCS invested in the prospects of future growth and generous financial returns in the form of the Quest for Excellence dividends.

Only sustained sacrificial efforts—especially by the determined faculty, staff and board members—would sufficiently empower the Quest for Excellence. But could we hold out until the Quest for Excellence began to pay dividends in the form of increased enrollment, tuition and contributions? Some feared that failure would sink us into a fiscal abyss from which we might never rise. For my part, although I occasionally questioned how, my spirit remained confident in the progressive disclosure of God's provision. "God's vision is never lacking His provision," I reasoned, "and God's vision always exceeds our biggest dreams."

Pay the Price

As God leads, be willing to sacrifice and give all toward the fulfillment of God's purposes. When God wants to stretch your faith, the process is often uncomfortable, even painful, requiring you to see and do things differently and seemingly unnaturally. It is not unusual for rational people to question your sanity if you are like Noah trying to build an Ark on dry ground; like Moses trying to lead millions of people across the Red Sea without even one boat; or like aged Abraham and barren Sara trying to have as many children as there are stars in the sky and grains of sand on the shore. Trust Him to take care of your needs and your reputation in pursuit of the vision. Take heed; the more vision God gives to you, the more you are responsible for accomplishing. As Jesus said, " . . . to whom much is given, from him much will be required" (Luke 12:48).

Chapter 22: 11

CHAPTER 5
THE POWER OF PRAYER

"It's amazing!"

The VCS administrative offices echoed with excited voices as the news spread about the letter that had just arrived. God was opening a door to a new site.

During the 1990–91 school year we received word that the Campbell Union High School District had decided to close Branham High School and put the property out for lease bids. VCS jumped at the opportunity because the spacious facilities offered a magnificent campus to accommodate the growth of both our high school and our junior high. Against all odds, Valley Christian Schools won a five-year lease, starting in the fall of 1991.

While our location at the Campbell Community Center had worked well for two years, it did not allow for expansion. We did not relish another move, but our new lease at the Branham site would guarantee at least five years of geographical stability for our junior high and high school students in a campus designed to meet their needs.

As I thanked God for this provision, I felt the familiar mix of exhilaration and trepidation that often accompanies a faith venture. No doubt we were proceeding in God's will, with much prayer coverage, but as we made financial arrangements over the coming days it became clear the Lord would need to continue to provide in supernatural ways. Our monthly campus lease payments would dramatically increase. With finances already tight, we borrowed funds to come up with the $45,000 lease deposit.

Our joy on opening day that September, however, overshadowed any anxiety about money, at least temporarily. The Branham campus also became home for the VCS administrative offices and allowed us more room and flexibility than we had enjoyed since our lease of the Camden High School campus.

One Monday evening shortly after the beginning of the fall semester, various events kept me on campus. By the time I packed up to head home, stars studded the dusky sky.

On my way down the hall toward the parking lot, I noticed a glow from one of the classrooms. *Somebody forgot to turn out the lights,* I surmised. When I opened the door to look for the light switch, however, I found four women and a man sitting at student desks.

Beverly and Dean Deaton, Paula Keith, Andrea Saltray, and Sheri Vavken — all parents of students — were praying for the VCS board, the administration, the faculty, the students, and the entire San Francisco Bay area. "Would you like to join us, Dr. Daugherty?"

I hesitated. My first thought — *This wasn't really what I had planned to do right now* — was quickly overtaken by a second: *The superintendent of a Christian school shouldn't decline an invitation to pray.* I smiled and slipped into a chair.

Soon I learned that Bev and Sheri had met weekly to pray for Valley Christian Schools and their neighborhood for several years. This was their first night to pray on campus. Since our move to Branham, they had felt an increased burden from the Holy Spirit to pray on site, and had gathered a core group of committed parents to join them in interceding for spiritual renewal at Valley. They sensed God's desire that VCS make a greater impact on its students and on the larger community. Further, they had a strong leading to pray for an awakening in the entire San Francisco Bay area that would begin at VCS.

As I listened to the fervent prayers of these parents, their earnest passion for a fresh outpouring of God touched my spirit. I knew Valley Christian Schools had always depended on the power of prayer to see God's will accomplished, but these intercessors had much to teach me. My next lesson came soon enough.

GOD SPEAKS THROUGH PRAYER

As fall moved into winter it became apparent the school had a major financial crisis looming. With higher lease and larger facility costs, VCS faced a projected $280,000 deficit for the school year. As superintendent, I felt very alone to face the challenges except for the highly supportive VCS board and the few faithful intercessors that met on Monday nights. Their appeals for other parents to join in prayer produced few if any additional prayer partners. But I was comforted by the determined intercession of our Monday evening prayer band. I sensed that God would turn the tide of red ink into a positive cash flow, because the "fervent prayer" of the righteous "avails much" (James 5:16), and because Jesus said, "For where two or three are gathered together in My name, I am there in the midst of them" (Matthew 18:20).

Call In The Air Force!

The Bible refers to Satan as "the mighty prince of the power of the air" (Ephesians 2:2). Although the enemy always opposes God's work, I have learned that He appoints prayer intercessors to call in air cover for His faithful warriors on the front lines. Watch for and honor the intercessors that God assigns to pray for you and the vision you share. . . .

Chapter 22: 14

As I prayed, the Lord laid out a three-step plan of action that came to my mind so clearly I wrote it down. Right away I talked with the VCS board and administrators and received their unconditional support. We scheduled an urgent meeting for all the parents of our students on February 20, 1992. The plan was bold, but I moved forward with confidence because I had no doubt of God's intentions.

Hundreds of parents gathered at the First Baptist Church that night. "I believe God is showing three steps He wants us to take, and God will provide the money that's needed," I explained. The room became quiet, and I felt tension and apprehension mounting as I struggled to continue. "First, Kris and I will sell our home in Elk Grove." (After moving we had kept our home as a rental.) "God has led us to donate the equity—which I think is about $70,000—to the school. Second, the VCS board has agreed to match our donation with their personal contributions totaling $70,000. Third, I'm asking parents and friends of VCS to match our combined $140,000 with another $140,000 to total the $280,000 needed."

People's stunned expressions sent a loud message. Some looked somber, others agitated. After my presentation I overheard comments that confirmed what I saw in their faces. Many seemed to be feeling, "Go ahead and sell your house, but I'm keeping mine. How did you get the school into such a mess?"

Their reactions were in stark contrast compared to the earlier reaction of my wife, Kris. After I realized what God was leading us to do, I made my first call to Kris and explained the whole plan. She questioned me: "Are you sure this is God speaking, or is this your idea?" I encouraged her to pray and listen for herself.

Later she responded, "I haven't heard from the

Lord about it myself, but I trust that you have." She was willing to give the equity in our only home even though she thought it improbable that we could ever put enough money together to buy a home in San Jose. The cost of housing in the Bay Area was skyrocketing and we had no savings. This sacrifice pained her, but Kris was willing to stand with me, and never complained. (Only a year later, as it turned out, God arranged incredible circumstances to enable us to move out of our small rented house in San Jose and purchase a house in Campbell. Several VCS board members contributed toward the down payment.) We still live in the same home that has more than tripled in value.

DARKNESS BEFORE DAWN

As God had assured me, commitments were eventually made for the entire $280,000 (more than the value of a three bedroom two bath house at that time) but it took some time before promised and intended gifts became money in the bank. The school's crisis took a turn for the worse a month later when the March 20th payday approached and we didn't have enough cash to meet payroll. The prospect of our poorly compensated, hard-working teachers and staff not getting paid was devastating.

The entire kindergarten through twelfth grade faculty and staff gathered for an emergency meeting in a science laboratory after school that Friday. "We took a step of faith in renting the Branham campus," I said, "and now we must trust God to supply the rest of the payroll."

To my astonishment and gratitude, no one was angry. Everyone expressed understanding and support. I invited employees to request checks for just what they needed to pay their bills and purchase food and fuel. Later I stood in the business office and watched as teachers calculated while waiting in line. Many did not ask for any money at all. Office manager Karen Baldwin and her staff processed checks for the amounts requested—and the school's bank balance lasted longer than the line. I thought of the promise, "My God shall supply all your need according to His riches in glory by Christ Jesus" (Philippians 4:19).

As soon as they learned of the payroll emergency, the intercessors sprang into action. Spontaneous prayer broke out among the Valley Christian Schools' community. I announced that the school's theater would remain open for prayer at any time during the school day. Many students, staff, and friends went to the theater to pray that God would release His provision. The faculty met together for prayer, and students interceded for them in the classrooms. We designated Tuesday, March 24, as a day of prayer, and asked everyone, including parents, to go to the Lord simultaneously at 9 a.m., wherever they might be.

After about a week, the immediate crisis was resolved. The three-phase appeal finally bore fruit. Sufficient funds came in from gifts and tuition payments to meet the payroll. Payday came late, but we were never more joyful as we gave thanks to the Lord for His faithful provision.

Moreover, the Lord turned the tide on our budget deficit. People began to open their hearts and respond to the call partly because they saw the unselfish sacrifices of the school leadership and board of directors to jump-start the flow of God's provision. They also saw how faculty and staff had willingly sacrificed for the sake of the school's ministry.

God did not fail to prove Himself. The money came in, and the deficit was fully covered. What an awesome experience to witness how the Lord answered and met our need.

LESSONS IN PRAYER

During those months I came to understand prayer at a deeper level. I had always seen prayer as vital and effective, but God began to open my eyes to the need for persistent, pervasive, and prevailing prayer.

Previously, my view about prayer went something like this: God is not deaf. He hears the first time we pray. He doesn't have a short-term memory problem, so there is no need for "vain repetitions" (which Matthew 6:7 condemns). One short, sincere prayer is all God needs. If our loving Lord knows "yes" to be the best answer, He will answer "yes." If not, we shouldn't be presumptuous and beg, as if God were too busy to hear the first time. If God didn't answer "yes" after the first prayer, it's because He said "no" for a good reason.

Another favorite verse I used to cite was James 5:16: "The effective, fervent prayer of a righteous man avails much." I reasoned that ganging up on God by asking other people to pray was pointless because numbers do not persuade God. The kingdom of God is not a democracy. He gives us the best answer the first time when even one righteous man prays.

With all that was occurring, I was challenged to study the Scriptures relating to prayer in more depth. My growing experience and new insights from my studies revealed an alternate perspective. I learned that intercessory prayer preceded deliverances of God's people for all the spiritual renewals described in the Bible. Further, the magnitude of the breakthrough was proportionate to the width and depth of prayer. The width of prayer refers to the number of believers interceding, and the depth of

prayer measures the fervor and persistence of their intercession.

A broad, pervasive prayer base—one that is representative of the body of believers—aligns with scriptural
teaching about the importance of unity and the church
operating as Christ's body. Having a wide number of
intercessors can make prayer more effective by coun-
teracting ungodly tendencies toward "hermit-minded"
Christianity, dissension, and a spirit of pride. The Bible
also shows many examples of people who prayed persistently over extended periods, including Nehemiah (Nehemiah 1:4) and Jesus Himself, who prayed for hours or
all night before key turning points in His ministry (Luke
6:12; Matthew 14:23–25, 26:36–44). I also realized that
some of Jesus' parables teach that persistent prayer may
be needed before answers come (Luke 11:1–13, 18:1–8).

AN ACTION PLAN FOR
SPIRITUAL RENEWAL

By 1992 I was having regular conversations with
Ed Silvoso, who volunteered as chaplain of the Valley
Christian Schools board of directors. For many years, Ed
and his wife, Ruth, had met weekly for prayer and Bible
study with four other couples: Carlos and Debbie Corona,
Bob and Carolee Luthie, Robert and Carol Wallace, and
Rick and Pam Watson. Rick served as chairman and Robert as vice-chairman of the VCS board of directors. All
five families had children enrolled at Valley and kept the
school in their prayers.

During the summer of 1992 Ed asked to get
together with me at a local coffee shop. "Cliff, I believe
God wants to use the strategic position of Valley Christian
Schools to help bring spiritual renewal to the City of San
Jose and the whole South Bay area," he told me. "Have

you thought about the extent of Valley's influence in the community? Our students represent more than 150 local churches."

I listened intently to Ed's words, because I knew how his Harvest Evangelism ministry had nurtured spiritual renewal in both North and South America. Extensive intercessory prayer provided the foundation for a three-year outreach in Resistencia, Argentina, that doubled the evangelical population of that city.

Ed shared an action plan he felt the Lord impressing on him that would set the spiritual agenda for renewal at Valley Christian as the first goal. Over the coming months we put most of his plan into action.

In August we held a retreat attended by all seven board members and five administrators to dedicate VCS and ourselves afresh to the Lord's purposes. Ed taught all of us about "spiritual warfare" at our "spiritual boot camp." About a month after school began, Ed led another two-day retreat for our administrators, faculty, and staff, with the same focus.

Then in November 1992 Ed arranged to send Kris and me to Argentina for the second annual Harvest Evangelism International Institute in Buenos Aires. At this gathering we had the opportunity to learn about transforming entire areas through prayer evangelism. We saw how intercessory prayer had a revolutionizing influence on many communities. This life-changing experience implanted a vision for spiritual transformation at Valley Christian Schools. Our faith grew with anticipation that God would bring a renewal at VCS to achieve all of His purposes.

LAUNCHING STUDENT INTERCESSION

Over the next couple of months I began writing what God was teaching me about prayer in a paper that became the basis for an initiative called "Pray Valley." My excitement rose as I saw the potential of this effort to impact our students, their families, the wider Santa Clara Valley, and possibly beyond.

Journal the Journey

Periodically document the ways God has supernaturally worked through your life. Honor Him for His faithfulness, and allow these accounts to bring you and others into a new dimension of faith and love of God.

Chapter 22: 20

On Wednesday, January 13, 1993, the senior high students gathered in a chapel service where I introduced Pray Valley. I felt specifically directed by the Holy Spirit as I spoke.

"The vision of Pray Valley depends on a band of student intercessors who will pray daily for every VCS high school student by name," I said. "We want to discover God-appointed student prayer intercessors to cover all students in prayer by name every day, at least through the Spiritual Emphasis Week this spring. Are you one of the intercessors God is calling?"

Within four weeks, fifty-eight student intercessors volunteered. The school's Bible teachers helped identify at least two or three pupils in every class who committed to pray for up to ten students and their families each day. The student intercessors also prayed for each other and their Bible teachers. Six adult intercessors prayed daily for the student intercessors. Student volunteers signed an Intercessor's Covenant, co-signed by their Bible teachers. The intercessors kept a prayer journal and contacted at least weekly the students for whom they were praying. They noted requests and answers to prayer in a prayer log.

By the time we gathered the intercessors together on Tuesday, March 9, to pray and hear reports, ninety percent of the 410 high school young people had student intercessors lifting them before the Lord.

The student intercessors shared what God had been doing in them and through them since the launch of Pray Valley in January. "It's been a struggle," one admitted. "I've been attacked spiritually, but it's drawing everyone closer together."

"My relationship with God has really grown," said another. "God is becoming more real."

Others rejoiced at how the Lord had powerfully answered prayer requests for fellow students and their families. Seeing results encouraged them and made them want to continue interceding.

As I listened to their testimonies, my heart was thrilled at the evidence of God working to bring spiritual renewal to the students at Valley Christian Schools. The intercessors prayed with sincerity for the Lord to touch everyone during the Spiritual Emphasis Week.

THE FRUIT RIPENS

On Friday, March 12, the last morning of Spiritual Emphasis Week, the high school administration scheduled a double, ninety-six-minute chapel that was to end at the 11:30 lunch bell. The entire high school student body attended.

The intensity of God's presence felt as if the entire

gym had become a spiritual sauna. A student worship team led in some praise songs. Then students were offered an open microphone to share from their hearts.

Several teens expressed grief for sinful actions or attitudes, repenting publicly and rededicating themselves to the Lord. Barriers crumbled as others asked for prayer about painful relationships, anger, grudges, and their desire to forgive friends and parents who had hurt them. Many times after a student spoke at the microphone, others stepped forward to gather around the speaker in support. Some who disclosed their own struggles invited others dealing with similar issues to come for prayer. They placed their hands on each other's shoulders and sought the Lord with deep emotion.

Board Chaplain Ed Silvoso was scheduled to speak but managed to squeeze in only a few sentences and an invitation: "The Holy Spirit is speaking to many of you now. If He is asking you to accept Jesus Christ for the first time, or if you want Him to help you to better understand God's Word, or if you want to submit your life more fully to God's Holy Spirit, I want you to come forward and kneel on this gym floor right now."

More than 150 students responded immediately, several bolting from their seats toward the front. I felt the bleachers vibrate, strain, and rumble, and I hoped no one would be injured. Before long, nearly everyone was praying throughout the gym—many kneeling or crying or hugging others.

When the lunch bell rang, no one left as the Spirit of God continued to move. I imagined how upset some parents might be if their teenagers didn't eat lunch. Toward the end of the high school lunch period I announced on the microphone that anyone who wanted lunch needed to leave "now." No one left. As the junior high lunch period began, I thought, *it's not a good idea to let high school students join the junior high lunch, but we don't have a choice.* I made another call for lunch—but again, no one left. They kept praying.

Toward the end of the junior high lunch period I was feeling desperate. How could I ever convince parents that their teenagers did not want lunch? I made a final appeal, saying, "This is the last chance for lunch!" But the high school didn't have lunch that day. The cafeteria workers waited in vain as the students fasted spontaneously. I imagined hundreds of unclaimed meals and confused cafeteria workers standing at their windows asking, "Why didn't somebody tell us there was no lunch today?"

Our lunch crisis reminded me of when the disciples admonished Jesus, "Rabbi, eat." But He said to them, "I have nourishment of which you have no idea . . . My nourishment is to do the will of Him Who sent Me and to completely finish His work" (taken from John 4:31–34, TAB). It became obvious: Jesus had served His own banquet to our students that day! After the students eventually vacated the gym, prayer continued all over campus.

Later, students tried to describe what the Lord was doing in their lives, but words seemed inadequate. "Things have really changed," one boy said. "God has put me on fire. I'm taking a stand in school now. I didn't have the courage before, but now God is giving me the strength."

Another told me, "What happened was a surprise and much greater than what we expected or imagined. All embarrassment went away. Students felt that it was more important to surrender to God than to worry about what their friends would think."

POWER FOR TRANSFORMATION

Thank You, Jesus! My heart filled in awe and gratitude as I reflected on the Spirit's work. Persistent and pervasive prayer was releasing the power of God to renew and transform our school. I sensed we had turned a corner in dedicating ourselves to wholehearted pursuit of the Lord Jesus—seeking His reign in our own lives, in our families, and in our community.

Within a week after the chapel I invited John Isaacs, a VCS parent and senior pastor of South Bay Covenant Church, to meet me for lunch. We talked about continuing the prayer emphasis throughout San Jose and the surrounding area. Soon a handful of key ministers and intercessors from the community began meeting weekly in my office to plan a new prayer outreach. Out of Pray Valley, the "Pray South Bay" movement launched in October with a kick-off banquet involving five local churches from diverse backgrounds and denominations. Susan Bagley, a VCS board member, was instrumental in helping to organize intercession and the kick-off banquet. Many leaders gathered in the VCS small gym on the first Thursday of each month to intercede for the region. Pray South Bay eventually expanded into "Pray the Bay" that focused on intercession for the entire San Francisco Bay area. Ed Silvoso played a lead role in nurturing these initiatives. They in turn fed into the Lighthouses of Prayer movement that swept the nation and beyond, with neighbors blessing neighbors through prayer evangelism.

Valley Christian Schools would never be the same. One of the biggest signs of God's guidance came as we ended the fiscal year in June 1993 with $50,000 in the black. Until then, VCS had not balanced an annual budget for more than a decade. We gave thanks for the work of Ken Dobbel, the school's CFO during the early 1990s.

Dan Burford, a VCS board member since 1988, introduced Ken to VCS. Ken Dobbel worked very effectively with Valley's vendors to negotiate payment plans and maintain the school's financial commitments during the early phases of the VCS Quest for Excellence™.

We gained the courage to raise tuition by more than fifteen percent for two successive years and eight percent the third year to balance the operational budget so that tuition could actually fund operations and slowly increase teacher salaries. With operations covered by tuition, contributions multiplied as donors were able to direct their giving to the Quest for Excellence to pay for better programs for their children. Gradually improving salaries enabled VCS to begin the long journey to attract and retain quality teachers more competitively.

Fears that increased tuition would push economically strapped families out of the school and suppress enrollment proved groundless. As tuition income funded higher quality, applications for enrollment increased beyond our expectations, enabling us to more selectively register outstanding students for our growing student body.

God worked through His praying people to birth the Quest for Excellence and prosper the ministry of VCS. We saw Him spiritually transform the lives of Valley's leadership, staff, students, and community. Now that our priorities for VCS were more aligned with His purposes, our days of budget deficits and crisis fundraising were finally behind us. We never looked back.

CHAPTER 6
HEMMED IN ON ALL SIDES?

Lord, how many hoops do we have to jump through? How much opposition do we have to face? It seemed as though the obstacles to a new campus on the hill cropped up at every turn.

Everyone at Valley Christian Schools called our land the Skyway property, after the name of the dead-end road that nudged the base of the hill on the southwest side. Even the term "dead-end road" seemed to speak volumes about our project. For five years after our purchase, the Skyway property laid dormant of all development as it provided habitat for the rare and endangered plants. Still, VCS had pursued work on the Environmental Impact Report (EIR), despite the seemingly improbable odds of building a school on the hill. The City of San Jose demanded completion of the EIR and other prerequisites before officials would even consider rezoning the land from residential use to a planned development for a school.

The EIR dealt with all the issues regarding traffic, noise, visual impact, and mitigation of airborne asbestos fibers from the serpentine rock during construction. David Powers of Powers and Associates, our consultant for the EIR, worked tirelessly to finish the report and fulfill all the requirements needed by the City Planning Department to evaluate our Planned Development Rezoning Application. Approval of this zoning change would permit joint development by VCS and South Valley Christian Church. Even though we couldn't see any workable solutions to the endangered plant situation, getting the rezoning approved with an eventual mitigation plan would allow us to take the next steps.

When neighbors of the Skyway property got wind that VCS and the church were moving forward with the rezoning application, several of them organized outspoken resistance. Some apparently did not want any development in their "backyard." Others seemed concerned primarily with the potential traffic hassles. Many made passionate appeals to the City Planning Department and the City Planning Commission, an advisory board.

As a result, the staff of the Planning Department recommended against granting permission for rezoning. The Planning Commission, in turn, voted unanimously to refuse the application. The City Council had ultimate authority over the decision, but I knew they seldom approved a proposal over the opposition of the Planning Commission and the City Planning Department staff.

Is this where the project will die, after all? I wondered. In spite of all circumstances, I still felt God had a plan for us to use this property. *"Lord, You have the final word, and anything is possible with You," I prayed.*

GOD CASTS HIS VOTE

In addition to the King of the Universe, Valley Christian Schools had one strong ally. Charlotte Powers (no relation to EIR consultant David Powers) had recently won election to the San Jose City Council, representing the district that included the Skyway property. She stood firmly in favor of rezoning our land, despite the opposition of neighbors and the contrary recommendation of planning officials. With Charlotte Power's support, VCS made an appeal to the City Council at their Tuesday night meeting on May 17, 1994.

For several tedious hours, school representatives and neighbors sat resolutely while the meeting dragged on with other agenda items. Finally the rezoning issue came up for discussion.

Charlotte Powers gave a powerful speech backing our request. "A fine school like this will have a wonderfully positive impact on our community," she asserted. She made a motion to approve the Planned Development Rezoning Application.

Some of the neighbors heaped fury on their new council member, but she held her ground. Another council member seconded her motion and made a similar complimentary statement about the value of such a project.

By the end of the discussion, the clock had ticked past midnight. Mayor Susan Hammer, also recently elected, called for the question, which required a six-vote majority for approval by the eleven-member council. Council members leaned forward to press the buttons that recorded their votes electronically for immediate display on the wall of the council chambers.

Gasps filled the room as people sat in stunned amazement. Despite the opposition by the City Planning Department, Planning Commission, and neighbors, our rezoning application passed unanimously.

My spirit soared all the way home. *Truly all things are possible with You, Lord,* I marveled. *You did have the final word, and it was YES!*

WHICH WAY NOW?

Getting our property rezoned to permit development of a school took us a major step toward our dream of a new campus. But it would remain nothing more than a dream, it seemed, as long as the endangered plants held highest claim to the land.

In 1995 Gerry DeYoung, our project-planning consultant recommended that we authorize David Powers, our EIR consultant, to conduct a special study of the rare plants. He wanted to know their numbers, placement, and growing conditions, in hopes of discovering a plan for a new school to coexist with them. Nothing seemed workable, but I acknowledged that God had already moved this project forward several times in the face of apparently hopeless odds.

Meanwhile, the school's board began wondering if it might be possible to sell the Skyway property and either purchase a surplus school or buy flat land where we could build without such overwhelming obstacles. Over the next year the school's executive team, with a directive from the VCS board, tried to locate such options. But in spite of the heroic efforts of Chancellor Claude Fletcher, nothing became available. And with the plants standing in the way of any major development, we weren't even sure how much we could get for our property. While uncertain of God's plan, I still felt strongly that the Lord had given us the land on the hill as His first choice for a new school.

By spring of 1996, the Monday night prayer meeting had become a beacon of light in my week—one of the only groups where faith for the development of the Skyway campus burned brightly. The intercessors called upon the Lord even more fervently for His direction and provision.

One Monday evening in early June, our prayer group met in my office on the Branham campus. Those attending included parents that I met in the classroom back in 1991: Bev and Dean Deaton, Andrea Saltray, and Sheri Vavken. Sheri's husband, Werner, had joined the group by this time. As we discussed the roadblocks to building on the Skyway property, the Holy Spirit birthed a thought in Werner Vavken.

"Cliff, I sense God speaking to me," he said. "I keep hearing Him say, 'Build a cross. Put it on the top of the hill. Claim the land as My hill and declare it as holy ground.'" The idea excited us and, we agreed to help.

CLAIMING THE HIGH GROUND

Within days Werner Vavken and his son Joe, a VCS alumnus, built a twenty-foot wooden cross and painted it white. The following Saturday afternoon, June 8, 1996, we drove to the top of the hill to erect the cross. The group included Werner, Sheri, and Joe Vavken; my son, Zane; and Ron Buchholz, another VCS alumnus.

The ground at the highest spot on the hill turned out to be hard rock, yet Werner insisted on planting the cross at the summit. While we stood perplexed, Werner discovered the stump of an old telephone pole in the rock, cut off near ground level. Sounding optimistic, he said, "I think we can dig around this pole's base, bolt the cross to the pole, and fill in the gap with concrete."

Our crew went to work. We had to connect three or four long hoses together to get to the nearest faucet for the water to mix the concrete. I buried a Bible, wrapped in a protective plastic container, at the foot of the cross. After praying to claim the land as holy to the Lord, we returned home to prepare for the formal dedication service planned for the next day.

On Sunday afternoon, June 9, members of the VCS board and Pastor John Isaacs gathered before the newly raised cross with several of the school's intercessors, including Andrea Saltray and the Deatons. Rick Watson and I, as VCS board chair and superintendent, stood as the legal authorities representing the ownership of Valley Christian Schools. We prayed and declared that God's perfect will and purposes should be accomplished on the Skyway property.

"Lord," I prayed, "let this cross and the Bible

planted here always testify that 'the manifold wisdom of God might be made known by the church to the principalities and powers in the heavenly places, according to the eternal purpose which He accomplished in Christ Jesus our Lord,'" quoting Ephesians 3:10–11.

During this gathering, I recounted how Kris and I had discovered the headless German shepherd on the crest of the hill during our walk back in 1990. We declared, "God's eternal purposes will be accomplished on the Skyway property, and if the enemy approaches this hill, he must face the testimony of this cross and the power of God's Word, the Bible."

We concluded with a communion celebration. After the Lord's Supper, everyone present expressed a sense that a great change had taken place in the heavenly realms. With the cross's erection as a kind of down payment for the construction of a Skyway campus, we felt that the Lord, in some special way, took possession of the hill that day. Our dedication of the land to God birthed fresh faith that something wonderful and powerful was going to happen.

A DEADLINE, A BREAKTHROUGH—AND AN IMPASSE?

Our renewed faith led me to call Gerry DeYoung, our project-planning consultant. I asked him to analyze possible options for building a school around the endangered plants. Was there any way to avoid or preserve their habitat and also construct the facilities we needed? The feeling still gripped me that God had some solution to our dilemma.

Then one day during summer break I was sorting through mail at my office desk when a page with the letterhead "Campbell Union High School District" caught my attention. The letter, dated July 15, 1996, notified us that the district was seriously considering reclaiming the Branham campus as a public high school by fall 1999. We had a lease extension that would allow us to remain on the site in the meantime, but if the school district pursued their plan, as was likely, VCS would have to pull up stakes before the 1999–2000 school year.

I felt my pulse quicken as I realized that our dream of a new campus, languishing for so many years, now took on urgency with a real-life deadline. With heightened anticipation I awaited the report from Gerry DeYoung.

After a few weeks of study, he called to go over the results of his analysis. He outlined several scenarios that could accommodate building a school around the rare plants, but all of them required using the developer's four acres of terraces that bordered Diamond Heights Drive on the northeast side of our hill. Although VCS held title to the whole property, the agreement we worked out during our purchase negotiations in 1988 still gave him the right to buy back, for $1.00, this land he wanted to retain for a development of town homes.

Encouragement and dismay fought for control of my emotions as I listened to Gerry DeYoung explain the proposals. Purchasing the terraces would settle access issues from Senter Road on the north side and resolve differences about building density that arose between the other owner, the city, and VCS. But I knew that another brick wall stood between such a purchase and us.

I was right. The developer had no interest in surrendering his claim to the terraces. He remained intent on building town homes, and would not consider a buy-out.

But in the weeks and months to come, the school's prayer support continued with intensity. We were convinced the challenges were no match for our Commander in Chief. Yet God alone knew how this battle could be won.

CHAPTER 7

GOD IMPARTS TO HUMAN HEARTS

The Monday night prayer group—and others were interceding for Valley Christian Schools—lifting persistent prayers to the Lord for a solution to our property impasse. The prospect of a mitigation plan that would save the hill's endangered plants while allowing construction of a new school motivated us to seek God continually for His will to be accomplished. Months passed, and the developer stood firm in his intention to build town homes on the terraces.

Then one summer day I received unexpected news from Claude Fletcher. The office was quiet that Monday, July 14, 1997.

Claude had just talked with him. "One of his out-of-state projects has problems and he has a cash crunch," Claude explained.

The wheels in my brain whirled into high gear. *Lord, is this the opening we've been praying for?*

Valley's chief financial officer, Ray Wans, was out of the office for a few days. I asked Karen Baldwin, the office manager, whether we could write a $125,000 check from our general account. She said we could.

Next I spoke with Chuck Reed, legal counsel for VCS, about drawing up a purchase contract. He advised that only a quitclaim deed was needed. He reminded me that when the school had purchased the land on the hill, we had made a separate contract with the seller that sidestepped the costly process of obtaining a lot-line adjustment. This agreement granted us title to his entire property west of Diamond Heights Drive. But it also gave him the right to "buy back" these four-acre terraces for just $1.00 in order to build town homes as soon as the city approved a development plan.

The strategy I felt God pulling together so quickly looked like this: The school would present to the owner the first of two checks purchasing the terraces at the same rate negotiated in our original agreement—$1.00 per square foot. At the same time he would sign a quitclaim deed releasing the school from the contract to sell back the land to him for one dollar. Because VCS already held title to the whole property and a lot-line adjustment had not yet occurred, the quitclaim deed could be prepared and the deal completed immediately.

On Tuesday I signed the check. Chuck Reed finished drafting the quitclaim deed within another day or so. By the end of the week, we were ready to present the developer with an offer we hoped he couldn't refuse. One complication: My daughter, Kristin, was getting married that Friday afternoon.

GO, OR NO GO?

Claude Fletcher, chancellor of Valley Christian Schools, called the owner and asked him to go to coffee on Friday. Claude took the check and the quitclaim deed with him and planned to close the deal.

Meanwhile, I prepared for my role in Kristin's wedding. I could scarcely contain my wide range of emotions at the union of my twenty-six-year-old daughter and Mike Annab. At the same time I could only hope and pray that God would move the owner to sign the quitclaim deed that would finally allow VCS to build on the Skyway property. After almost nine long years, alternately hurdling one obstacle after another and waiting in tedious limbo, we seemed to be on the brink of realizing the dream of our own new school.

After driving to the wedding reception from his meeting with the owner, Claude caught up with me. I saw the smile on his face before he spoke.

"He signed!" Claude declared. "He took the money and signed our quitclaim deed. He'll deposit the check today." Our agreement promised him a second check for $50,000 covering the balance of the purchase price for the four acres at $1.00 per square foot.

The elation of the wedding and the good news from Claude overwhelmed me all weekend. With this property, VCS could move ahead with planning the construction of the campus. The terraces would later become the location for six tennis courts.

The next week, however, a phone call from the developer to Claude Fletcher put question marks around the deal. He had second thoughts and wanted to rescind our agreement. The two met again for coffee to discuss his concerns.

Later Claude described to me their conversation. He told the seller that he doubted the VCS board would want to undo the transaction. Besides, the school couldn't put a stop-payment order on the check, because it had already cleared the bank. He concluded it was too late to back out. As a consolation, Claude agreed to get an understanding from the VCS board to sell the terraces back to him at cost if VCS did not use the land to build a school. Of course, we had every intention of building, God willing!

Thanksgiving and a sense of awe for God's extraordinary provision overflowed from the intercessors, our board, and our leadership team. With this purchase we had the land to move forward while avoiding construction that would harm the endangered plants. I now understood why we could not get the lot-line adjustment nine years earlier. Having title allowed our purchase to go forward quickly with the quitclaim deed, releasing these crucial four acres for our use.

MOVING THE MOUNTAIN

With the bulk of the hillside land at last under our control, the VCS administration huddled with the consultant we had hired to implement the mitigation plan preserving the endangered plants. Contracting with Dr. Niall McCarten had been another divine blessing. During the spring of 1997, Chuck Reed, legal counsel for VCS, had learned that a new professional associate of his was acquainted with members of the California Department of Fish and Game, which oversees habitats of sensitive species of both plants and animals. These state officials could suggest firms they thought might assist the school. Through his associate, Chuck received a short list of recommended firms to carry out a mitigation plan that Fish and Game would likely approve.

Dr. Niall McCarten of Jones & Stokes, an environmental planning and management firm, was at the top of the list. Claude made the contact. Dr. McCarten said he could solve our problem and agreed to develop and implement a plan for only $10,000. Compared to earlier price tags of $200,000 to $300,000 eight years earlier, Dr. McCarten's bid seemed too good to believe. Yet his work proved to be a blessing from God.

Niall McCarten collaborated with Gerry DeYoung, our project planner, to determine exactly where the proposed school buildings would be located so the area could be cleared of plants. Just as the mitigation plan was moving toward its last stages, we received official notification that Campbell Union High School District intended to reopen the Branham campus as a public high school by fall 1999. In fact, they aimed to reclaim part of the campus starting in fall 1998 during a planned refurbishment. The clock was ticking down on our lease. Soon our junior high and high school students would need a new home.

By the last day of December 1997, we finished carrying out the mitigation plan, and the endangered plants had their new home on the hill. The Metcalf Canyon Jewelflower and Dudleya flowering plants were moved from the construction zones to a newly created Dudleya Preserve located on a portion of the Skyway property not slated for development. Chancellor Fletcher led the project. Armin McKee and his daughter Amy (VCHS, 1995) drove their bulldozer and tractor to move almost one hundred cubic yards of serpentine rock for the new preserve. Lance Kilpatrick (VCHS, 1998) and my son, Zane Daugherty (VCHS, 1991), worked for two weeks removing and replanting each of the plants by hand.

Only later did I learn just how key a role Niall McCarten had played. He might have been the only consultant able to persuade State Fish and Game to approve this plan, because Dr. McCarten was the person who had originally convinced both the state and federal governments to list the plants as endangered.

A PRAYER OF FAITH

As we moved past New Year's Day 1998, I could still see a mountain of challenges that demanded resolution before a school could rise from the hill. First on the horizon came the VCS board of directors meeting on Thursday, January 8. The board was still uncomfortable with the numerous difficulties presented by the Skyway property. By all reasonable measures, the project seemed impossible to even the most seasoned developers. Many board members still preferred to abandon the hill, sell the property, and use money from its sale to buy elsewhere. The breakthrough with the endangered plants had not released all doubts and fears. Surely, some directors believed, there were less difficult options than transforming a mountain into flat construction spaces for the buildings and athletic fields.

I was frustrated. *"Lord,"* I prayed, *"I can't convince this board that You want to build on the hill. If I am not hearing from You, please release me from this vision. If You want to build on the hill, You are going to have to convince the board Yourself."*

During my preparations for the January board meeting, I felt an unusual prompting to write down a prayer. The words began to flow:

"Our Heavenly Father, there is no doubt of Your great works in the founding and building of Valley Christian Schools. We, as Your servants, are privileged to walk with You. Your mighty provision and power are evidenced in the creative work You are doing in the lives of over 1500 students and their families. In times past You have shown Your perfect timing and provision. . . ."

The prayer then recounted several miracles God wrought in arranging for new sites and bringing needed funds. It went on:

"Now, Lord, we continue to see Your mighty work, Your great provision, and Your perfect timing. You are opening the door to build a new campus on the Skyway property. You were planning for this new campus long before we understood Your purposes. . . . May all of our

hearts be strengthened by Your long record of faithfulness in providing for Valley Christian Schools. Lord, we claim these Your promises, which we sense are given to us for this project at this time." I then cited several scripture passages the Lord had impressed on me.

At the January 8ᵗʰ board meeting, eight members attended along with the three members of our executive team, including Chancellor Claude Fletcher, CFO Ray Wans, and me as CEO, President/Superintendent. At the beginning of the meeting I brought out the written prayer and invited board members to take turns reading and praying through it together. While passing a copy of the prayer to every person in the room I realized that I had never before brought a written prayer for our board. A strong sense of God's presence invaded the room. The passages of Scripture they read aloud in the prayer included these:

"The God of heaven Himself will prosper us; therefore we His servants will arise and build" (Nehemiah 2:20). "Enlarge the place of your tent, and let them stretch out the curtains of your habitations; do not spare; lengthen your cords, and strengthen your stakes . . ." (Isaiah 54:2–4). "But he who puts his trust in Me shall possess the land, and shall inherit My holy mountain" (Isaiah 57:13).

The prayer ended with this declaration: "Your kingdom come and Your will be done at Valley Christian Schools as it is in heaven. In Jesus' mighty name, Amen!"

> **Let God Speak for Himself**
>   Do not be surprised when you cannot convince others to support a God-sized project. After all, a rational person would immediately say that any of God's plans seem impossible. Trust that He knows how to communicate with people who are needed for the project in ways that are personally meaningful to them.
>
>   Chapter 22: 10

GOD HAS SPOKEN

The prayer had a dramatic effect on everyone present. Each board member read portions in succession until everyone said, "Amen!" Some fell to their knees during the reading. Clearly God had spoken: "Don't be afraid. Move forward. I'll build the school!"

The Lord had transplanted His faith as a gift into the heart of every person in the room. Before the meeting's end, the board formed a new building committee with Vera Shantz as chair. Other members included Mike Beever, Dan Burford, and Don Watson. Steve McMinn, Chairman of the Board, walked out to the parking lot with me that night and affirmed that he felt that God would build the school on the hill. It was such an encouragement to me.

Within days, however, Valley Christian Schools received another dose of bad news. Word came from the San Jose Planning Department that VCS needed to reapply for a zoning permit. Evidently the quitclaim deed on the developer's former property had triggered this requirement.

Well, OK, I thought. *It shouldn't be that difficult, right?*

It shouldn't have been, but there was one snag: The

City of San Jose accepted General Plan amendments only during November of each year, and any rezoning application that differed from a project's General Plan could not be approved without a General Plan amendment. But November was ten months away—and VCS had no time to lose. Sitting on our hands during such a delay would make it impossible to build the school before we lost the Branham campus.

The Monday night intercessors turned up the heat. With our ageless, omniscient, and almighty God standing outside the timeline of human affairs, this turn of events was not a surprise to Him nor too hard for Him to handle.

It only *looked* like another insurmountable obstacle.

CHAPTER 8
TICKING CLOCK
OR TIME BOMB?

"Oh, no—February 2? I'm going to be out of town!"

When I heard the date the City of San Jose had chosen for Valley Christian Schools to meet with the City Planning Department, I knew I would have to pray from a distance for God to accomplish His will. Other trustworthy representatives of the school would attend the crucial meeting without me.

With the endangered plants now safely out of the way, our executive team and the VCS board felt an urgency to move ahead with our plans for construction. We needed city approval for every step and could not afford any delays if we hoped to have the new campus built before we lost our lease at Branham. Now the city was telling us we needed to reapply for a zoning permit and a General Plan amendment. This requirement would put our building project hopelessly behind schedule.

On Monday, February 2, 1998, I was attending a Pastors' Prayer Summit at Mt. Hermon Conference Center, twenty-five miles southwest of San Jose. I prayed for God's favor upon the VCS representatives attending the city's meeting: Chancellor Claude Fletcher; Chuck Reed, our attorney; and Gerry DeYoung, the project planner. At 3:30 p.m. they would meet at City Hall with Carol Painter, the acting deputy planning director. Claude set up the meeting through the office of Jim Derryberry, planning director for the City of San Jose and a friend of Claude's from the time he had served on the City Council.

As the time approached, I prayed together with Reverend Susan Bagley, an insightful prayer leader who also served as vice chair of the VCS board. For half an hour we interceded for the meeting and its participants. Then at 3:30 I found a place by myself to pray and meditate on God's Word.

Stay in the Book
Feed your soul on God's written Word. Maintain high regard for God's ability to guide and direct through the eternal principles of Scripture. Memorize passages so God can use them to speak to you at any time.

Chapter 22: 2

The Lord brought His Word alive to me as I pondered and prayed about His plans for Valley Christian Schools. In what seemed like only about ten or fifteen minutes, God directed me to specific powerful passages of Scripture as fast as I could turn the pages of my Bible. I was so moved by His presence that I wrote "2–2-98" beside each passage that spoke to me about our school circumstances.

Later I had opportunity to write a description of what the Lord impressed upon me through these verses to share at the next VCS board meeting.

PROPHETIC WORDS FROM SCRIPTURE

When I got the phone call reporting on the school's meeting with Carol Painter of the San Jose Planning Department, the news made my heart leap for joy and gratitude. The city would not require a zoning change. Evidently our plans conformed to the use already approved. In fact, Carol Painter advised VCS to go ahead and apply for a Planned Development Permit, the master permit needed to implement the zoning intent. As it turned out, Jim Derryberry, at Claude's request, had reviewed the zoning issue and concluded that VCS did not need to rezone its property.

Journal the Journey

Periodically document the ways God has supernaturally worked through your life. Honor Him for His faithfulness, and allow these accounts to bring you and others into a new dimension of faith and love of God.

Chapter 22:20

At the March board meeting I gave the directors the document I had written to describe what God had shared with me at the prayer summit about what He would do to build the school.

The message was so detailed that unless it was from God it could not be 100% accurate. The risk of being labeled a "false prophet" hovered in my mind, but God had given me such faith that I could not help but share what I had heard. I felt the reality of "the substance of things hoped for," as Hebrews 11:1 defines faith. Only time would validate whether these declarations came from God, when He brought them to pass—or not.

Each faith declaration was backed by full references to the scripture passages God had given me. (Although I had read and marked my King James Bible at the Prayer Summit, I quoted from the New King James in writing this document.) In condensed form, here is what I reported to the board:

The Lord assured me that He will work miraculously to build His school for three primary purposes:

     1. Then you shall know that I am the Lord (Ezekiel 36:11b).

     2. Then the heathen . . . shall know that I, the Lord, have rebuilt the ruined places and planted what was desolate. I, the Lord, have spoken it, and I will do it. . . . Then they shall know that I am the Lord (Ezekiel 36:36, 38b; see also 2 Chronicles 6:33b).

     3. Bring My sons from afar, and My daughters from the ends of the earth. . . . I will pour My Spirit on your descendants, and My blessing on your offspring . . . You are My witnesses (Isaiah 43:5–6; 44:3, 8b).

- In spite of the seemingly impossible task to build the campus, we are not to fear. The Lord is with us. (See Isaiah 41:10–13.)

- God formed Valley Christian Schools as His servant and He will not forget His servants. (See Isaiah 44:21.)

- Jeremiah prophesied that the children of Israel would be in captivity in Babylon for seventy years. The Lord prophesied two hundred years before Cyrus was king that after the seventy-year captivity, Cyrus would decree that the temple be rebuilt in Jerusalem. As prophesied, the powerful Babylonian nation was overpowered by a new nation, Persia. In the same manner that the Lord worked through the civil authority of King Cyrus of Persia to make the decree to build the temple in Jerusalem, the Lord will work through the civil authority to build the new Valley Christian Schools campus. If necessary, God will put down and raise up authorities to accomplish His purposes. During prayer, the Lord assured me that just as He declared that He would rebuild the temple, He is now declaring that He plans to build a campus for Valley Christian Schools. (See Isaiah 44:28, Jeremiah 25:11–12, Ezra 1:1–4.)

- The Lord will provide His resources to build the new school through both the generosity of His people and the secular resources of neighbors. (See Ezra 1:5–6.)
- God's people gave freely according to their means to the building project. The Lord will also move His people to build the new campus. (See Ezra 2:68–69.)
- God will unite our VCS family to build a new campus just as the people united as one man to build the temple to overcome major obstacles. (See Ezra 3:1.) As the builders laid the foundations, the people offered praise and singing to God. (See Ezra 3:10–11.) The local adversaries of the work attempted to join the work to defeat the project. (See Ezra 4:1–3a.)
- Our project is God's work and not our own. He will do His work through His people with His power as long as His people proclaim that "The God of heaven, He will prosper us; therefore, we His servants shall arise and build. . . ." (Nehemiah 2:20). God's enemies succeeded in stopping the construction of God's temple because the leaders of the project appealed only to King Cyrus's secular authority for building the temple rather than to God's authority. The builders also did not understand that they would fail if they tried to do God's work alone. God's work is God's work and not man's. The builders of the temple could not build alone" and neither can we. (See Ezra 4:3b.)
- We are battling the enemy for the soul of every young person who will ever attend Valley Christian Schools' new campus. Only God knows how many thousands or millions of souls are dependent upon the successful construction of our new campus. With so many souls

in the balance, it is certain that the enemy will do all he can to stop our progress as well. Because Zerubbabel appealed only to the authority of King Cyrus and not to the God of heaven and earth, he became helpless against the spiritual attack of the enemy. King Cyrus's temporal authority was no match for the powerful spiritual attack of the enemy. As a result, the new king, Artaxerxes, stopped the work. (See Ezra 4:21–23.)

- We must quickly learn what took Zerubbabel fifteen years to learn. The work to build the temple stopped for fifteen years! How confused and discouraged Zerubbabel must have become. He no doubt wondered what happened to the prophecies of Isaiah and Jeremiah. He was certain that God had given them the command and provisions to build. God even spoke through King Cyrus. What went wrong? He prayed and wondered if he misunderstood all that had happened or if he had personally failed God. Was all lost? Would the temple never be built? He wondered and pondered these questions for one, two, five, ten, and even fifteen years. (See Ezra 4:24.)

- The fifteen-year delay became a spiritual warfare workshop for Zerubbabel. What he took fifteen years to learn must be learned immediately by all of us who are building Valley Christian Schools' new campus. Some of the lessons that Zerubbabel learned are as follows:

  1. So he answered and said to me: This is the word of the Lord to Zerubbabel: "Not by might nor by power, but by My Spirit," says the Lord of hosts. "Who are you, O great mountain? Before Zerubbabel you shall become a plain! And he shall bring forth the capstone with shouts of 'Grace,

grace to it!'" Moreover the word of the Lord came to me, saying: "The hands of Zerubbabel have laid the foundation of this temple; his hands shall also finish it. Then you will know that the Lord of hosts has sent Me to you. For who has despised the day of small things? For these seven rejoice to see the plumb line in the hand of Zerub-babel. They are the eyes of the Lord, which scan to and fro throughout the whole earth" (Zechariah 4:6–10). Note: When we view God as the only One who can prosper His work through our hand, we His servants may "arise and build." Then the eyes of the Lord will scan to and fro throughout the whole earth to protect His servants. As we are faithful to God's service, the Lord will "curse the thief" and "expel the perjurer" that will come against His work (see Zechariah 5:3–4).

2. Thus says the Lord of hosts, saying: "Behold, the Man whose name is Branch! From His place He shall branch out, and He shall build the temple of the Lord; yes, He shall build the temple of the Lord. He shall bear the glory, and shall sit and rule on His throne" (Zechariah 6:12–13). Note: The Branch is Jesus Christ.

3. Even those from afar shall come and build the temple of the Lord. Then you shall know that the Lord of hosts has sent Me to you. And this shall come to pass if you diligently obey the voice of the Lord your God (Zechariah 6:15). Note: We must obey the Lord by giving Him the glory for His power and His work.

4. Thus says the Lord of hosts: "Behold, I will save My people from the land of the east and from the land of the west; I will bring them back, and they

100 DR. CLIFFORD E. DAUGHERTY

shall dwell in the midst of Jerusalem. They shall be My people and I will be their God, in truth and righteousness" (Zechariah 8:7–8). Note: This speaks of bringing people to the Lord from all over the world.

5. Thus says the Lord of hosts: "Let your hands be strong, you who have been hearing in these days these words by the mouth of the prophets, who spoke in the day the foundation was laid for the house of the Lord of hosts, that the temple might be built" (Zechariah 8:9). Note: This message to the board is a foretelling of what God will do. When all looks impossible, remember that God has shown you in advance what He will do so be strong and do not despair.

- God's work must be under the spiritual authority and covering of God's spiritual leaders. The construction of the temple was put back on track when Zerubbabel received the help of the prophets. During recent years, the Lord has established such a spiritual covering for Valley Christian Schools. Weekly and monthly prayer meetings and the entire Pray the Bay movement are centered on campus. This spiritual covering is a gift of God and a protection that is critical to the success of our construction project. (See Ezra 5:2, 5.)

- After Zerubbabel applied the lessons he learned during his fifteen-year workshop on spiritual warfare, the Lord protected the project from the attacks of the enemy until the temple was completed. King Darius even donated some of his tax revenue to the project. God will make similar provisions for our project. (See Ezra 6:7–12.)

CAUGHT IN THE MIDST OF A FEUD

The VCS board members received this word as from the Lord. To the glory of God, their response seemed to mirror how the Jews replied to Nehemiah: "And they [cf. the board] said, 'Let us rise up and build.' So they strengthened their hands for this good work" (Nehemiah 2:18, KJV).

The building committee began its work by selecting a contractor, Richard Furtado of South Bay Construction, and a construction management team. Now the race against time was on.

Then, unbelievably, another roadblock arose: A squabble between two governmental authorities threatened approval of our building project. The City of San Jose had recently come to a standoff with the California Department of Fish and Game regarding projects the city favored. The State Fish and Game, which had authority over endangered species, would not approve added projects until the city met certain requirements with which the city did not wish to comply. As a result, all projects involving rare and endangered plants faced gridlock because of the unresolved issues between Fish and Game and the City of San Jose.

The city scheduled the first review of our Planned Development Permit Application for the morning of April 10, 1998. But as the date approached, Carol Hamilton of the San Jose Planning Department notified VCS that unless the school obtained a letter of clearance from the State Fish and Game signing off on the endangered plant mitigation work, the city would have no choice but to put our construction plans on hold.

What now, Lord? I wondered. *This is out of our hands—it's up to You!*

Chancellor Claude Fletcher contacted Niall McCarten, the expert who had overseen our plant mitigation project, and asked for his help in obtaining a letter of clearance from Fish and Game. Dr. McCarten told Claude he had personal contact with a member of State Fish and Game and was confident he could get the needed document. Carol Hamilton, on the other hand, expressed her doubt that anyone could wring such a letter out of Fish and Game given their tension with the City of San Jose.

A NAIL-BITING COUNTDOWN

The days ticked by with no sign of the clearance letter. When Claude Fletcher tried to follow up with Niall McCarten, his office reported that he was "in the field." Later, Dr. McCarten's return call brought the news that the person whom he had contacted to write a letter was ill and had also gone on vacation. He again promised to obtain the letter by April 10.

Still waiting and hoping, I entered my office that morning expecting to see the letter on top of my desk, but it had not yet arrived. I stole an anxious glance at the clock. Our meeting with the city to review the school's Planned Development Permit Application was to start at 10:30. Quickly I arranged a conference call with Claude Fletcher, Niall McCarten, and myself, and received another assurance that the letter would arrive by fax shortly.

At 10:15 the fax machine whirred to life, and soon disgorged the precious document. Immediately I sent it back through the machine to Carol Hamilton's office at the Planning Department, just in time for our meeting. The VCS representatives at the review told me later about her surprise at this resolution to the problem. Our project was still alive!

Moreover, within days Dr. McCarten confirmed that not only was the State of California signing off on our plant mitigation plan, but the U.S. Fish and Wildlife Service also had no further requirements at the federal level. Their formal clearance erased all doubts that this issue was finally resolved—more than nine years after our purchase of the property. Claude Fletcher e-mailed the VCS board on April 14 to report the good news: "This endangered plant issue was a very big hurdle to get over, and we are now over it—thank the Lord!"

At the next Monday night prayer meeting the intercessors rejoiced and gave great thanks to God for His awesome provision. Still, as we recalled the 10:15 fax arrival, some of us remained a little breathless at how close God had cut it this time. *What a cliffhanger!* I thought, shaking my head at all the amazing things we had experienced with the Skyway property. *How many more cliffhangers would we face to build this one school?*

CHAPTER 9
PUTTING THE PIECES INTO PLACE

After nine years of deadlock, our solution to the endangered plant predicament seemed only to incite fresh neighborhood opposition to development of the Skyway property. At stake was the size of the project. By 1998 Valley Christian Schools had grown to serve a combined total of almost 1,100 students in the junior and senior high schools and envisioned more each year. Further, neighbors who objected to the potential traffic impact seemed intent on blocking the school's construction by any means possible.

Charlotte Powers, the City Council representative for the district of San Jose that included the Skyway property, called a community meeting for Tuesday evening, May 12, 1998, to hear the concerns of the neighbors. VCS Chancellor Claude Fletcher, a former City Council member himself, recognized the importance of such a meeting and the school's efforts to put its best foot forward. If angry neighbors turned the tide against the new campus, we could be forced to reduce student capacity to the point where the project might not remain cost-effective.

The intercessors took the matter to the Lord. In addition, VCS made every effort to develop positive relationships with the neighbors. Claude began going from door to door in the area to talk about our plans for the campus, and I joined in the effort.

A home at the corner of Skyway Drive and Stoneyhaven Way would experience the greatest traffic impact from the new school, so we very much wanted its residents not to oppose the project. On Saturday, May 9, I approached this home about seven o'clock in the evening as I went "doorbelling" in the area. Walking across the driveway, I prayed silently with each step, *"Lord, Your will be done."* When I reached the house I knocked on the front door and felt my pulse pick up pace with the sense that God is in control and He wants to get this school built!

The door swung open and a smiling face greeted me. "Hello, Dr. Daugherty!" the man said. "Come on in. What is happening with the new school project?"

With wonder I replied, "Actually, that's what I've come to talk with you about."

As I entered the home, the man continued, "I don't know if you know us, but we know you. I'm Dan Smith," he said, also introducing his family, who had gathered to see who was visiting. His wife, Janet, held their four-month-old baby, while three older children hovered nearby. "Jan and I taught Spanish at Valley Christian High School years ago, before you became superintendent. Then we started our own business, and God has prospered us. Now it turns out this home we bought is near where the new school will be built. We are thrilled!"

I could hardly believe my ears—yet in a way I wasn't the least bit surprised. "Well," I answered, "you may not realize how providential it is that you bought this home."

Dan had heard of the Tuesday evening community meeting with Charlotte Powers, but had made other plans for that night. "Since I don't oppose the school, I didn't think I needed to attend," he said.

After I explained how crucial his public expression of support could prove, Dan agreed to change his plans and come to the meeting.

All heaven must have heard me say *"Thank You, Lord!"* as I left the Smith home that evening.

A HEAVEN-SENT ADVOCATE

The following Tuesday evening, several dozen people gathered at a local intermediate school as Carol Hamilton from the Planning Department called the community meeting to order. Charlotte Powers led the discussion, and several other officials from various government agencies were present to hear the remarks.

As we had feared, many neighbors made strong comments about their sense of betrayal four years earlier when Charlotte Powers and the City Council had approved the school's Planned Development Rezoning Application. They reminded listeners that the Planning Department and Planning Commission had both opposed the project from the beginning. They expressed concerns about the traffic analysis from the Environmental Impact Report that predicted between 6,000 and 7,000 daily trips to and from the school—up and down Skyway Drive. Further, they said their children's safety would be at risk from teenage drivers "racing" through their neighborhoods as they cut through their otherwise "quiet" residential streets. They also decried the school's potential adverse effect on their property values.

The negative tone of the meeting concerned me, although I kept praying silently throughout the succession of speakers. Many other Valley Christian supporters, I knew, were interceding both in the audience and from a distance.

Dan Smith had not yet said a word. Then, after a short break in the comments, he rose from his seat with his baby in his arms and young daughter nearby.

"I live at the corner of Skyway and Stoneyhaven

Drive," Dan began. "You probably know that my house will be more impacted by added traffic than any other home. I have children, too, and I'm very concerned about their safety. Like others who have already spoken, I believe the city should take steps to protect our children by making some changes to our traffic flow.

"However," he went on, "I'd like for everyone to look at this project from a different point of view. We should be thankful that such a successful college-pre-paratory high school is moving into our neighborhood. I consider it a privilege that Valley Christian Schools is moving next to my home. I don't think my property value will decline. If anything, it will increase. I, for one, want to welcome Valley Christian Schools as our new neigh-bors!"

The room fell silent for a few moments as listeners reflected on Dan's words. From that point the tone of the meeting changed. The issue of whether Valley should pro-ceed with building a new campus in the neighborhood was not discussed again. Instead, neighbors began to express ideas about how to make the project compatible with the residential area. By the meeting's end, I sensed their ani-mosity level was significantly reduced, amid reassurances that Valley Christian Schools would make every attempt to be a good neighbor.

Dan and Jan Smith proved to be heaven-sent advo-cates for the new campus. Their ownership of the house at Skyway and Stoneyhaven was no mere coincidence. With joy and thanks, the intercessors added another mar-vel to the growing list of all God had done on behalf of the school. [1]

"NOT A SPARROW FALLS . . ."
We hardly had time to savor this victory, however. Two days later Valley Christian Schools received a let-

ter following a procedural inspection required by the city, with news that gave many of us chills. Incredibly, another rare and endangered species had taken up residence on the hill. A single male burrowing owl and his den were found on the Skyway property near its border with Danna Rock Park. State Fish and Game law required that land within 250 feet of the burrow remain undisturbed until after the owl's nesting period, when the bird could be legally relocated, or until the owl moved voluntarily.

Although the owl's burrow lay on the portion of the hill property planned for construction of the future South Valley Christian Church facility, the grading and earth-moving of the entire plot of land needed to take place at the same time.

Frustration swept through the VCS community when the news spread. Concern about delays in excavation prompted some serious suggestions that "the owl might have an accident." Others with a slightly more compassionate approach proposed putting a tennis ball into the burrow to force the owl to move.

Although I, too, was taken back by this discovery of the latest endangered species on our property, I sent an e-mail to the VCS board and several others who were by now working on the project, trying to reassure them. "Nothing escapes the eye of God," I reminded them. "I believe the project is still on God's timeline."

I cautioned that no one should try to remove the owl outside of Fish and Game guidelines. "Such action would indicate we believe we must take matters into our own hands rather than trust that God has all within His hands. We must have faith that our Lord who sees every 'sparrow that falls' has carefully planned all matters related to the owl and our project schedule."

I also expressed concern that anyone disturbing the

owl's burrow illegally might cause the bird to move to a more central part of the construction site, creating more trouble.

To encourage those at risk of despair, I recounted the story of how God had recently proved His faithfulness through the providential placement of Dan and Jan Smith. I wrote, "If God put Dan and his family in the most strategically located home next to our new school 'for such a time as this,' I am confident that He has not 'accidentally' overlooked the location of the owl's home. Let's all 'keep the faith' and remain faithful in our efforts as we prayerfully move forward with confidence."

Over the coming weeks I tried to nurture an atmosphere of quiet trust. The intercessors kept this situation before the Lord, and the building committee pursued work on approval of our Planned Development Permit.

After a couple of months, VCS received a written report from the naturalist who was patiently monitoring the burrowing owl. The report described the demise of the owl by "a natural carnivorous event." All excavation restrictions were lifted.

FILLING IN THE HOLES

Meanwhile, another obstacle had arisen the previous winter when it became obvious that the girls' softball program was in trouble. The engineers at Ruth and Going had successfully plotted locations at the Skyway campus for all sports except girls' softball. The site simply needed more flat space.

The only solution that looked possible involved the purchase of an approximate two-and-a-half-acre property that came to be known as the "donut hole" because it was nearly surrounded by our Skyway site. Gerry DeYoung, our project planner at Ruth and Going, advocated the purchase of the "donut hole" along with construction of an eighty-foot wall. The wall was to be located next to Diamond Heights Drive to retain about one third of the football field. This additional land would allow the football field to turn northward on its west axis to make room for the softball field.

Chancellor Claude Fletcher investigated ownership of the "donut hole" and determined that a police officer and his wife lived in their home on the property. They did not want to sell their home because he planned to retire from the police department in about three years and preferred to stay put until then.

Nonetheless, I felt convinced that God would somehow open the door to purchase this piece of land to provide for the development of the softball field. Without girls' softball, VCS could not offer a comprehensive program to attract students and serve families. Again, the intercessors took the matter to the Lord.

One morning in May 1998, I was reflecting on this situation with the Lord. *"Lord,"* I prayed, *"we need the officer's property to build the softball field, but he isn't willing to sell it to the school. I know You have planned for a comprehensive high school so construction of a softball field is absolutely critical. You need to do something about this real soon! We need your guidance. If we delay much longer, the huge retaining wall for the football field will be built and then it can't be moved. We'll be stuck without a softball field."*

An overwhelming sense of God's presence became very real. In my spirit I heard Him reply, *"You're very concerned about the school's needs, but you should be just as concerned about the officer's needs. Why don't you consider his needs as well as the school's?"*

I paused to think about this and then continued the

conversation. *"OK, Lord, that's a good point. But what needs should I be concerned about?"*

"Consider," God impressed upon me, *"what will happen to their property value after the high school marching band starts practicing. They will be playing on the football field just behind his home each summer and fall for four months. You have an ethical obligation to make him whole. Tell him about this problem and offer him about ten percent over the fair market value of his property to help with his moving expenses and real estate fees."*

My eyes widened at this new thought. Later that day, I explained to Claude Fletcher what I understood God to say. Without delay, Claude approached the officer, explained the concerns about the marching band, and offered to purchase his property for ten percent more than its fair market value.

"Well, I'll need to talk this over with my wife," the policeman responded.

Three days later he called us back to accept the offer. We made all the arrangements and concluded the purchase on May 20, 1998. Shortly thereafter, the policeman and his wife relocated to a new home.

God seemed to be putting pieces into place, but the biggest barrier still loomed before us: Where would VCS get the money to build?

CHAPTER 10
HOW BIG IS YOUR FAITH?

I gulped as the numbers hit me again. Obtaining funds for an endeavor as big as the construction of the Skyway campus appeared as challenging as an ascent on Mount Everest by a Girl Scout troop on its first day hike. Valley Christian Schools, now debt free, had about $1.2 million in the bank and owned the Skyway property outright. But estimates ran from $10 million to $12 million just to excavate and build the retaining walls required to re-contour the hill for the building pads, dirt roads, and barren athletic fields. All this work was needed before "normal" construction could even begin.

Valley Christian Schools' recent experience with long-term fundraising did not afford much optimism. VCS was in the final months of a capital campaign to establish the Teacher Endowment Fund, and it took VCS ten years to reach that fund's $1 million goal. Nevertheless, with a leap of faith, the building committee bravely set an initial three-year capital campaign goal of $4 million—raised to $5 million by the campaign's official launch—for the new campus. Chancellor Claude Fletcher and CFO Ray Wans accepted the challenge but, they told me, not without some "fear and trembling." Many of us found that the frequency of our sleepless nights and the seriousness of our prayers increased dramatically.

During the spring of 1998 the building committee members began to realize what the school would cost to construct as the details came into focus. The numbers were frightening. Quickly they launched a reevaluation of the project and reduced the scope of Phase One from more than 200,000 square feet to just less than 150,000 square feet. Even after this reduction, estimates for construction continued to grow.

Ray Wans' first analysis of the school's loan service capabilities indicated that VCS could afford to borrow between $15 million and $18 million. The Evangelical Christian Credit Union where we held our general account suggested that a loan of $12 million to $13 million best fit our situation. After I spoke to the contractor, however, a cold gloom began to take hold of me.

I voiced my concerns at our weekly building committee meeting. "I believed the school could handle a $12 million to $13 million loan. I began to believe the school could manage a $15 million commitment. Later, my faith stretched to $18 million, and then to $22 million. But when I heard from our contractor, Richard Furtado, that we need a $25–28 million loan, my heart sank. No matter how I've calculated or how I've prayed, my faith hasn't stretched past $22 million."

Many people felt exactly the same way. Yet in such circumstances one cannot help but continue to pray, no matter how hopeless the situation looks. Before long, an idea came to me that allowed my faith to stretch to $28 million.

FROM WHERE DO RESOURCES COME?

Increased enrollment would mean more tuition income, giving VCS a financial base to handle a bigger loan. The margin on any added revenue would be high since the lease costs remained reasonably priced. One day as I walked the Branham campus, God gave me fresh eyes to see the abandoned and deteriorated industrial arts wing. If we could renovate and use this facility for new classrooms, we could enroll more students.

I petitioned the Campbell Union High School District for VCS to rent this wing for the last year of our lease. Because the district was planning to reopen Branham as a public high school in the fall of 1999, their facilities director viewed our occupation of the industrial arts facility as a step in the wrong direction. But after Claude Fletcher spoke with district representatives, VCS gained permission to lease it.

The building was a mess. Our hard-working facilities staff cleaned the space and divided several areas into new classrooms. With a tremendous effort by everyone, including Bob Bridges, junior high principal, and Curt Willson, high school principal, VCS was able to boost enrollment from fewer than 1,100 junior and senior high students to almost 1,300. The added students represented an annual revenue increase of almost $2 million, and moved our enrollment projections ahead at least one year. Now we could foresee more than 1,400 students moving onto the Skyway campus.

Armed with new data, CFO Ray Wans embarked upon his search for a $28 million loan. To our dismay, however, the bankers' faith had not stretched along with ours. Their questions reflected their doubts: "What happens if you don't get all of the city approvals to build the school before your lease runs out? You could be out on the street with 1,400 students, and then how will you repay the loan?"

The bankers' objections continued: "The school's capacity to repay the loan depends on continued revenue growth from about two hundred new students during the next two school years. What happens if enrollment growth is less than projected at the Skyway campus? Are you sure you'll have the same enrollment demand at the school's new location? If not, how will the school make the loan payments?"

Even with Ray Wans' heroic efforts, our best hopes for a loan seemed to hover between $18 million and $20 million. But such an amount would not enable us to finish construction—and without a completed facility VCS would not be able to pay off the loan.

From all appearances, the magnitude of the project alongside the limitations of the school's resources put us at another impasse. But in the face of what looked like impossible circumstances, the intercessors continued to pray. At our Monday night prayer meetings we sensed God's assurance that He was building the school with His resources rather than those of VCS. We often reflected on the promise in Philippians 4:19, "And my God shall supply all your need according to His riches in glory by Christ Jesus."

A GATEWAY OPENS—WITH
A TOLL TO PAY

The countdown to closing of the Branham campus was sounding and the only alternatives were "build or bust." I knew each member of the VCS board of directors was also interceding for the needed resources.

As board member Mike Beever prayed, the Lord led him to some ideas that deserved careful study. After investigation, he introduced financial advisor Josh Cooperman to the executive team with the thought that VCS, as a non-profit 501(c)(3) corporation, could qualify for a tax-exempt, low-interest municipal loan.

We listened to the concept and agreed that it seemed to have merit. But at that time not one evangelical Christian school had ever received tax-exempt funding. Breaking new ground looked like a long shot. Yet VCS needed creative—even supernatural—help, and we concluded that such a loan might be God's solution to our funding crisis.

Josh Cooperman began his analysis of Valley Christian Schools' operations, working with a legal firm that specialized in tax-exempt municipal bond instruments. The firm evaluated VCS policies and corporate documents to determine if VCS was eligible.

After a few weeks a letter arrived outlining the findings. I scanned it and read the good news — the school qualified! Attached to the letter was a document describing some operational changes VCS would have to make in order to receive the funds. In addition to restricting prayer in school and meeting other criteria, VCS would have to drop requirements that:

- teachers be Christians
- board members be Christians
- employees sign a statement of faith
- students take a Bible class
- students attend weekly chapel

In short, to use tax-exempt, low-interest bonds, Valley Christian Schools could no longer remain Christian. At the next board meeting, we did not need further review. The board shared one mind: It would be better to close the school than to compromise the foundation of faith upon which the school rested.

Other members of the VCS community could not see any other way forward. I heard some argue that it made more sense to accept the criteria so we could run a thriving, quality private school rather than to close completely. By then God had blessed VCS significantly through the Quest for Excellence™. Faculty salaries and benefits had almost doubled since the beginning of the Quest. We had launched outstanding athletic and performing arts programs, with well-equipped classrooms and leading technology. The quality of students was rising steadily, as reflected in their achievement test scores. Should we sacrifice all of this on the basis of simple faith that God would miraculously finance a Christian school?

The school leadership stood firm. We agreed that if God chose to keep the doors open, He could provide the needed resources in His way. Our future was in His hands alone, because it was clear that only a sovereign work of an omnipotent God could meet the funding requirements to build the Skyway campus.

EXCAVATING BY FAITH

In July we learned that the City of San Jose had approved our Planned Development Permit Application, the master permit allowing us to implement the rezoning plans. We rejoiced at this progress, but day-by-day the clock's ticking grew louder. Little more than thirteen months remained until the end of our lease at Branham and no funding was in sight for a $28 million loan to build the Skyway campus.

Meanwhile, our contractor, Richard Furtado of South Bay Construction, had done some of his own praying and pressed ahead. Along with Ruth and Going, the engineering firm, South Bay Construction had succeeded in obtaining the grading permit to excavate and prepare the site. Massive retaining walls would support the relocation of approximately 600,000 cubic yards of dirt and rock to allow for roads, parking lots, building pads, and athletic fields.

In August, South Bay Construction broke ground at the Skyway site. On Thursday, August 20, 1998, the VCS principals and executive team abandoned our first administrative meeting of the school year and boarded a van to witness this milestone. Claude Fletcher and I snapped dozens of photos. As we watched a huge bulldozer moving the first load of dirt, I realized we were no longer

"Building the Dream," as we had titled our original capital campaign in 1989. We were now building the school!

Before long, Richard Furtado and his company had spent $10 million of their own money on the grading, retaining walls, and related work. VCS and South Bay Construction had yet to develop a contract because a loan to pay for this work was not yet in view. I feared Rich Furtado was placing his entire company at risk with no guarantee of payment, and I expressed my concerns to him.

His response warmed my heart. "Cliff, you are not the only person God talks to. God talks to me, too. The only way this school has a chance of getting built on time is to get started. We'll get the money."

I rejoiced at this exercise of supernatural trust in the Lord's provision. Richard Furtado had at least $10 million worth of faith.

Keep the Faith

Do not allow obstacles to stop you or to damage your faith. Your faith will soar if instead you see obstacles as opportunities for God to demonstrate His miraculous power. Let Him reassure you about His desire and intention to accomplish His highest purposes in whatever way He chooses. Remember that faith is a gift of the Holy Spirit, and until God gives us the gift for each of His works, we cannot manufacture the faith.

The Spirit gives special faith . . . (1 Corinthians 12:9 NLT).

Chapter 22: 15

CHAPTER 11
THE ULTIMATE ENGINEER AND MATHEMATICIAN!

"It just can't be done—we can't satisfy both sides!"

The crowd in the conference room at the offices of Ruth and Going, the engineering firm, kept crunching figures and brainstorming solutions. I listened closely as Gerry DeYoung of Ruth and Going, water systems consultant Eric Sitzenstatter, and about a dozen other consultants from different firms wrestled with an issue that had ballooned out of control since the early stages of planning—how to provide water for fire safety on the Skyway campus.

Consultants originally suggested that the new campus would require a water tower of close to 200,000 gallons to provide the pressure and volume needed to combat a fire for two hours at 1,200 gallons of water per minute. By 1994, the Environmental Impact Report recommended a tower at least twice as big in order to supply approximately 3,000 gallons per minute for two hours. Now, after four more years, new regulations indicated a need for roughly 4,500 gallons per minute for four hours—entailing a water tower with a fire-fighting capacity of 1,080,000 gallons.

The size and height of such a tower presented an engineering nightmare. No one seemed certain how it could be built safely, while everyone agreed it would cost millions of dollars. The city's fire department insisted on a tower because, officials explained, "Gravity hasn't failed us yet. Pumps are subject to mechanical failure."

Fire personnel would not settle for a smaller water tower, but the San Jose Planning Department vetoed such a huge and unsightly structure on top of the hill.

This issue looked like a "show stopper." The experts in the conference room expressed enthusiasm for the school's construction project. But as they talked I heard a contagious discouragement infect one person's comments after another. Even the best consultants could not figure out how to obtain enough water pressure to meet the "fire flow" requirements and avoid an intolerable visual impact.

BLUEPRINTS MADE IN HEAVEN

While the conversation continued, I listened reflectively. The engineers and consultants reached the same conclusion—we were at a stalemate.

With a hopeful determination that must have come from God, I asked, "I know you're the experts, and I'm sure you have no doubt considered what I'm about to ask. What about a water reservoir, rather than a water tower? The water would be present at the top of the hill. It seems like a reservoir could provide a reliable source of water for fighting a fire."

Gerry DeYoung commented, "You mean a swimming pool."

"Yes," I answered. "If we must spend millions of dollars on a water tower that would be needed only in case of a fire, it seems that we could put the money to better use by building an aquatics center that also serves as a fire-fighting system."

"Conceptually the idea is good," an engineer replied, "but the problem is that the pumps could come on automatically at any time in a fire emergency. Anyone in the pool at that time might be sucked to the bottom and stuck to the drain. That's why we haven't recommended the idea."

I could not let it go. "How about engineering a solution to this problem?"

The conversation stopped while people shifted in their seats and rustled papers. "The problem is very complex," one explained. "The chances of discovering a solution are very slim. Besides, if a solution doesn't exist, we're not into doing work that won't benefit the client. There's a little matter about getting paid."

A confidence I could attribute only to the Holy Spirit gave me resolve. "I believe a solution does exist. We haven't come this far on this project to meet failure now. Would your firm work on a remedy to this problem if we have a contract that stipulates you will be paid for doing the engineering work even if a solution can't be found?"

Some of their expressions told me they were still doubtful and apprehensive. But they agreed to make every effort to engineer a fire safety reservoir that could double as a pool, as long as I understood that a solution was unlikely.

Some weeks later, we met again. This time there were smiles all around the room as the engineers made their presentation. We were thrilled to receive the solution, along with their invoice for payment. As far as anyone knew, nobody had ever constructed such a pool. But it was feasible. A huge pool could function as a water tower. The plans included four-by-six-foot drains for the pool, gravity, and a combination of primary and backup diesel pumps supplying 4,500 gallons of water per minute.

I beamed as I heard their report. "You know, as time goes on it's becoming obvious: We're not developing the plans for the Skyway campus. We are discovering the plans that God has already drawn in heaven."

FAITH FOR AN AQUATIC VISION

When Coach Bob Colyar heard about the pool solution, he said, "I told you that God wants this pool in Phase One!" His joy reminded me of the faith he had exercised back in 1993 when he first approached me with his dream to establish a swimming and water polo program at Valley Christian High School.

My initial reaction had been cautious. At that time Valley fielded an otherwise full range of athletic teams with only 410 high school students. "Our athletes are spread thin now," I told Bob. "The football team has only about forty players for both varsity and junior varsity teams. Besides, we don't have a pool. The timing doesn't seem right. Let's let the school grow a bit more before we begin a swimming program."

Bob was ready for me. "I've already made arrangements to rent the pool at Willow Glen High School. With your approval we can do this. I'll be the coach, and I guarantee new students will come to the school. We won't pull from the other sports. There are swimmers all over this valley who would come to VCHS to participate."

He was right. By 1998 the swimming and water polo programs involved 150 students, and an emerging constituency of "aquatic parents" was asking where the pool would be located on the new campus. I told them about our funding challenges and explained that the educational facilities had to take priority. Pool space was planned, but construction would come in a later phase.

Bob Colyar and the other swimming parents simply prayed. He told the building committee, "I believe God wants to build the pool in the first phase. I just know He has money for this pool. I don't know how He will do it, but just wait and see. Plan the space for the pool and watch what happens."

Bob never suspected that governmental and engineering problems with a mammoth water tower would force the search for a pool solution. But he and the aquatic parents were thrilled when they heard the engineers' plan. And to top it off, estimates to build the pool came in lower than the cost to construct the water tower. With rejoicing and thanks to God, we submitted the plan to the San Jose Fire Department for its approval.

What I learned through this experience was a bigger lesson than that we needed the aquatic program. I finally realized that commitment to developing a comprehensive school was a key principle in growing a large, high-quality school. I learned that we must build the programs to attract students and not just try to attract students so we could build the programs.

Develop a Comprehensive Christian High School Committed to the Quest for Excellence™ in Every Area: The Whole is More Than the Sum of the Parts

Develop outstanding programs to attract students—don't wait until enough students are enrolled to justify the program.

Provide all program offerings normally associated with outstanding secular high schools, but insist that each program offer qualities that parents can find only through your Christian school.

Chapter 18: 2-A

TEN FEET TOO SHORT?

Meanwhile, another issue arose that pitted the needs of the swimming advocates against those of the baseball contingent. Nothing could be resolved without getting everyone together, so we called a meeting in October 1998.

The people around the conference table in the South Bay Construction trailer looked like they were ready for a showdown. On the right side sat Coach Bob Colyar and the pool supporters. On the left sat Coach John Diatte and others from the baseball program. The engineers clustered on the far end. Everyone looked intently at me seated at the head of the table, with Chancellor Claude Fletcher to my immediate right. I invited each side to restate its case.

Gary Radonich spoke for the baseball group. "Let me affirm that we're all in favor of a quality pool, and a fifty-meter pool is the ultimate. There isn't a fifty-three-meter pool in all of Northern California. The problem with a fifty-three-meter pool is that it shortens the baseball field by ten feet. The baseball program won't be able to host CCS playoffs if we have to give up ten feet of our field to allow for a 'super pool.' We need our ten feet back." Gary referred to the Central Coast Section of the California Interscholastic Federation, which oversees statewide high school athletic programs.

Bob Colyar explained his point of view. "I don't know who allowed only fifty meters for the pool, but I've been telling everyone through the entire pool planning process that we need a fifty-three-meter pool to allow for dual school and community use. The pool chemicals will cost more than $150,000 per year, and the only way we can fund that is through community use fees. If you take three meters off the pool, you'll need to add at least $150,000 to the annual pool budget."

I looked at the engineers sitting at the other end of the table. "There's got to be a way to accommodate both programs without compromising either one," I said.

Gerry DeYoung replied, "This plot plan was laid out long before we heard anything about a fifty-three-meter pool. We really squeezed to fit the fifty-meter pool into the plans, and the pool only recently became a viable part of Phase One. None of our engineers could have imagined that the school would want to build a 'super pool' larger than any pool in Northern California."

He went on, "It really comes down to simple math. There are only so many feet between the gym building and San Ramon Drive. We are ten feet too short to build both the 'super pool' and the CCS baseball field. The school needs to tell us which it wants."

Considerable debate ensued. Finally, I spoke up again. "It's not 'either/or.' These plans were made in heaven, and God's plans are never ten feet too short. There is an answer that accommodates both programs without compromise. We just haven't discovered it yet. Our engineers need to sharpen their pencils, go back to the drawing board, and figure this out."

An engineer who had helped design the San Jose International Airport replied, "You can't be serious! We can't add space that's not there." He opened the plans again, pushed a scale toward me, and insisted, "You measure the space and tell us what we've missed. The gym building and San Ramon Drive won't move. Show us where you get both a baseball field and a fifty-three-meter pool. We can go back and study this all you want, but nothing will change. This is simple math!"

FINDING A TRIANGLE

The room was quiet, as was I. For several moments I looked at the plans and prayed for divine guidance. I felt certain there was something there we hadn't seen.

Stretching for possibilities, I asked, "Who owns that triangle of land that juts into the baseball field?"

Someone answered, "That's the end of San Ramon Drive, and that's county land. We can't get that from the county."

"Claude," I asked, "would you check out the title on that property? There is something we've missed here. We need ten more feet and I believe it's here someplace."

Claude agreed to make the inquiry, and the meeting ended.

A couple of days later my assistant interrupted me with what seemed like a routine call. "Claude Fletcher on line two."

"OK, I have it," I answered.

Claude's voice sparkled. "I found your ten feet. In fact, I found fifteen feet! It turns out that our neighbor Tom DeHart, not the county, owns the triangle of land— Tom didn't even know he owns it. I talked to Tom and he was very agreeable. He's willing to sell the triangle to us for $1,000 to make the baseball field work."

"Wow! That's amazing!" I replied. "What generosity. He could have gotten much more."

"He's really a great guy and just wants to help."

Well, I reflected, *it really is true: Plans made in heaven are never ten feet too short!*

God did it again. His desire for excellence in both aquatics and baseball created a marvelous solution that would benefit VCS students and our community.

The clock seemed to be running quickly now. Campbell Union High School District had already reclaimed part of the Branham campus and was in the process of refurbishing it for its public high school students. On the backside of the campus, almost nine hundred Valley Christian High School students squeezed into congested modular buildings and the former industrial arts wing. Nearly four hundred junior high students, meanwhile, moved into transitional locations. The sixth graders went to Foxworthy Baptist Church and the seventh and eighth graders held school at South Valley Christian Church. The churches and the Campbell School District were very generous about space although our presence definitely inconvenienced them. Our teachers also suffered with less than ideal circumstances, but the students flourished. Without the churches' shared facilities and the district's extended lease and shared campus, Valley Christian Schools would have closed.

Through all of the supernatural answers to prayer for the launch of the Skyway campus "ship," God had cleared the decks of obstacles and set our course. With contractor Richard Furtado already at work, the ship had now left the dock, full speed ahead. But there was still no loan in sight to fund the journey through construction. Would VCS founder on the rocks?

CHAPTER 12
BUT GOD SAYS YES

The urgency to find a loan pressed on us like a steadily squeezing vice grip. Richard Furtado of South Bay Construction was moving ahead with grading and re-contouring of the Skyway campus site, and Valley Christian Schools already owed him millions of dollars. More than 1,500 junior and senior high students, employees and their families trusted the Lord, the superintendent, and the VCS board that the new school would be built on time. As the complexity of the project became more evident, we often reflected on the promise and the warning of Psalm 127:1: "Unless the Lord builds the house, they labor in vain who build it."

Board member Mike Beever and financial advisor Josh Cooperman had not given up on the idea of a tax-exempt municipal bond financing strategy. It seemed that only such a loan would come with a low enough interest rate for the school to afford the needed $28 million. During the summer of 1998 Josh submitted a detailed pro-spectus on the project to more than seventy national and international lending institutions that could fund a $28 million loan. Not one institution expressed interest in our project. Even worse, I feared that we could not accept a tax-exempt funding offer if one came, because we would again refuse to compromise our mission.

One day the phone rang in my office. Stephen Taber introduced himself as a municipal bond counsel with the San Francisco law firm of Hansen Bridgett.

"I heard from Josh Cooperman that Valley Christian Schools needs tax-exempt construction funding for $28 million," Steve Taber said. "I think I can help the school obtain such a funding on the basis of a recent Supreme Court ruling."

"That's good," I replied, "but did Josh also tell you that the school is not willing to compromise our Christian values in order to obtain the loan?"

After considerable discussion, I received a commitment from Steve that his firm would not force VCS to abandon its mission. He explained that he believed a new decision of the U.S. Supreme Court opened the door for "funding without compromise."

"Valley Christian Schools could become the first evangelical Christian school in the nation to obtain low-interest, tax-exempt bond funding if you would be willing to test the Court's recent ruling," he explained.

The idea sounded intriguing, although I remained leery of any avenues that might erode our Christian values. Steve Taber agreed to serve as bond counsel to help find funding for the project.

MOVING INTO THE RED SEA

Later the school called a special board meeting to consider the matter. Josh Cooperman made a strong appeal to the board to authorize the tax-exempt funding for construction.

I wanted to make sure he clearly understood our position. Because I knew of Josh Cooperman's Jewish faith, I explained that the deep principles of the board and school leadership mirrored the kind of unswerving convictions held by familiar Old Testament characters.

"You'll remember," I said, "the three young Hebrew men who chose to endure the fiery furnace rather than deny their faith and Daniel, who maintained his faithfulness to God even when it meant being thrown into a den of lions."

Josh reflected for a moment before answering. "God doesn't want you to deny your faith or compromise the mission of the school. But VCS needs tax-exempt funding. A taxable loan won't work for the amount of money you need. Dr. Daugherty, your devotion at the beginning of this board meeting quoted Moses as he and the Israelites stood before the Red Sea with Pharaoh's army approaching behind them. Moses' idea, as you mentioned, was that they should 'Be still and see the deliverance of God.' But you pointed out that God replied instead, 'What are you doing standing still? Start moving!' The way I see it, Valley Christian Schools is standing before the Red Sea. We can't just stand still; we must start moving!"

Then it was my turn to reflect in silence. While I had prepared that devotion, I hadn't thought about its full significance in view of the decisions at hand. It began to make sense. Neither the children of Israel nor Moses knew how God would part the Red Sea when Moses raised his rod. The VCS board, for its part, did not know how tax-exempt funding could be arranged while avoiding compromise. Yet the message seemed clear: *Move ahead and let God part the Red Sea.*

Before the meeting ended, a motion was made, seconded, and passed unanimously. The board directed me to obtain tax-exempt bond funding without surrendering the mission of the school.

Mission Impossible?

Don't dismiss "impossible" options. Likewise, do not assume that the opening of promising new doors means that God wants you to walk through them; pray and ask God to confirm His direction.

Chapter 22: 8

GOD HONORS CHRISTIAN VALUES

Steve Taber proved very helpful in the process of evaluating the school's constitution, bylaws, policies, and contracts for wording that might trigger a violation of the First Amendment. As I worked to rewrite the documents with the advice of legal counsel, I sensed the supernatural leading of God in walking a fine line.

The key was for all documents to present VCS as a non-profit, public benefit Christian school serving a secular educational function in the context of "the Judeo-Christian values of the Bible as reflected in the life and teachings of Jesus Christ." This phrase became the legally accepted means by which the school distinguished itself as an educational institution founded on Christian values rather than as a church school. As an independent Christian school, VCS was well positioned not to violate the First Amendment's "establishment of religion" clause but entitled to enjoy the "free exercise thereof" guaranteed by the same amendment.

Meanwhile, three lending firms that finally expressed an interest in funding a $28 million loan quickly narrowed to two. These were the only lenders willing to consider what they believed to be an enterprise loan, based on revenue projections as opposed to a proven revenue history.

After considerable analysis and interpersonal communications, the lending organization presented a signed term sheet that Valley Christian Schools accepted. The tax-exempt rates were negotiated to nearly four percentage points lower than conventional market rates. This meant that the annual interest payments we would make to service our $28 million loan would have bought us a loan of only $17 million at a conventional rate of interest.

The lenders required a bank-approved appraisal, and when I received the report my faith climbed to yet a new level. The appraised value of the land and Phase One of the Skyway project came to $39.5 million. I felt transformed from a "Lord, I believe; help my unbelief" Christian into a "Wow! I'm amazed!" Christian (see Mark 9:24).

LOOKING FOR A CHANNEL

It looked as though the Red Sea had parted, but Pharaoh's army was still advancing and we had a long trek ahead to cross the sea on dry ground. To complete the requirements of the tax-exempt bond issue for construction of the school, VCS needed a municipality to serve as a conduit for the bond. In effect, a local government entity would qualify for and receive the tax-exempt bond. Then the entity would step aside and Valley Christian Schools would accept the bond proceeds—and the responsibility for repayment—to finance the approved non-profit, public benefit project.

VCS Chancellor Claude Fletcher was busy working on options for such a conduit. As a former San Jose City Council member, he hoped his contacts would encourage the City of San Jose to help us by taking this role. Our council representative, Charlotte Powers, and at least one other council member supported the effort. Steve Taber, as our municipal bond counsel, joined Claude for our presentation to the city, but the city attorney was convinced that serving as a conduit for a $28 million bond issue for Valley Christian Schools would violate the First Amendment clause forbidding a government "establishment of religion." The city attorney stood firm against a persuasive presentation by Steve Taber.

Not deterred, Claude called several of his friends on

the Santa Clara County Board of Supervisors and asked for their support. Supervisor Blanca Alvarado, board chair, offered to do what she could, but said the county counsel would have to review, approve, and recommend such an action to the board. Claude arranged for a meeting, but, to our dismay, the county counsel held the same opinion as the city attorney.

No other options seemed promising. Prayer intensified for a breakthrough. The intercessors knew that only God could make the difference.

Steve Taber asked the county for an opportunity to provide a written legal opinion explaining why the recent decision of the Supreme Court had opened the door for the county to receive a conduit bond of $28 million for Valley Christian Schools. The county counsel agreed to review his written opinion, while prayer continued. After close study, the county counsel changed course and agreed to give our project a favorable recommendation to the Santa Clara County Board of Supervisors.

My excitement grew as safe passage across the Red Sea began to loom in our sights. As required by law, VCS provided a two-week notice in the local newspaper inviting people to express their views on this matter at a public hearing scheduled for late September 1998.

On the appointed day, the Board of Supervisors assembled in their chambers. The chair of the meeting opened with the Pledge of Allegiance, and then invited those present to comment about the county's proposed sponsorship of a $28 million municipal bond on behalf of Valley Christian Schools. No one stood. Within thirty seconds the public hearing was closed with the bang of a gavel. Directly afterward a motion was made, seconded, and unanimously passed. The Santa Clara County Board of Supervisors went down in the history of public funding in America by sponsoring the first municipal bond issue for a non-profit evangelical Christian organization.

THE POWER OF UNITY

With each hurdle vaulted, our hopes rose, but we were still not out of the Red Sea. All county bond funding passed through the nine-county Association of Bay Area Governments (ABAG) and ABAG's Finance Authority for Nonprofit Corporations. The decision of Santa Clara County would have to be ratified by legally appointed representatives of the nine counties. The liberal reputation of many governmental agencies in the San Francisco Bay area made the region one of the most unlikely places in the United States for a faith-based organization to gain the necessary support for municipal bond financing. Moreover, because of the precedent-setting nature of our case, the ABAG staff wanted a unanimous decision.

The hearing was scheduled at the ABAG offices in Oakland on October 1, 1998. VCS sent a team of administrators, lawyers, and consultants, including Steve Taber. Waiting for proceedings to begin, I glanced at my watch. The meeting was late—the chair had not called it to order on time. *What's wrong?* I wondered.

Before long the representative from Santa Clara County came to apologize for the delay. It seemed that not all the county representatives were in agreement, and the chair apparently did not want to start without unanimous consent.

I sat and prayed for God's will to be done. The verse came to my memory, "The king's heart is in the hand of the Lord" (Proverbs 21:1a). Ten, fifteen, then twenty minutes passed.

While waiting I also reflected on the development of the Lighthouses of Prayer movement that began out of

the 1993 revival chapel service at Valley Christian High
School. Scores of churches had since launched thousands
of Lighthouses of Prayer in the homes of Christians who
committed to pray for their neighbors. During the weekend just before the ABAG hearing, a great breakthrough
had occurred: Churches in the last of the nine counties in
the San Francisco Bay area had joined the "Pray the Bay"
effort to establish Lighthouses of Prayer in every county.

Thirty minutes had passed since the meeting's
scheduled start time. Occasionally we got an update
passed to us from our Santa Clara County representative. As I considered our pending situation with ABAG,
I mused about a possible parallel. *Could it be that establishing Lighthouses of Prayer in all nine counties had to
take place first? Was this another example where spiritual
renewal and deliverance of God's people is preceded by
broad intercessory prayer?*

After forty-five minutes, the board members filed
into the room. The tension among them suggested that
only God knew how the final vote would go.

When the chair brought up the proposed $28 mil-
lion municipal bond from Santa Clara County for Valley
Christian Schools, one of the board members spoke.

"I'm not in favor of approving a $28 million non-
rated bond," he said. "This isn't the way we should be
doing business. This bond is not only non-rated, it may be
in violation of the First Amendment."

Steve Taber then spoke and addressed the concerns.
When he finished, the representative responded firmly.

"I am opposed to this funding," he repeated. "But
given the circumstances surrounding this issuance, I'm
going to vote for it this time. I'll never vote for such a
funding again. I vote only with the understanding that the
board will meet later today and draft a policy to disallow
such approvals in the future."

The team from VCS sat in silence while the motion passed unanimously. With relief and awe, I felt the tension begin to subside. *Thank God!* I expressed silently.

Later I learned from Claude Fletcher that even more had been going on behind the scenes than was apparent. In the days prior to the scheduled hearing, Claude and others had contacted all ABAG board members about the VCS issue and only one expressed adamant opposition to the proposal. Since the VCS proposal was unique, ABAG staff wanted the issue to be approved unanimously. In part because of Claude's efforts, the dissenting member decided to be "unavailable" for the meeting as an accommodation to that objective. "Unfortunately," Claude said, "we spent some very anxious moments before the meeting began waiting for the staff to make personal contact to confirm that the member was not planning to attend."

In light of this news, the unexpected opposition expressed by another member during the meeting made his eventual approval all the more amazing. I could see that Claude's advance work had also helped prepare our Santa Clara County representative to champion our cause to the other members during the meeting's delay.

As I had often reflected on how God has used Claude in such circumstances, I repeated to myself, *Thank God for Claude*.

LEFT IN THE LURCH?
The exhilaration we felt lasted for days. Introducing a phrase we would quote more than once, our Jewish financial advisor, Josh Cooperman, noted, "You know, it seems like 'a miracle a day' around here."

The funding of our $28 million funding was in sight. We needed only for Hansen Bridgett and the lending corporation to finish drafting all the documents for signatures.

The bubble burst when Josh Cooperman phoned to inform me that the executive general counsel of our lender was requesting a conference call. About fifteen people were to take part, including the VCS executive team and legal counsel as well as the lenders' senior vice presidents and legal counsel. Immediately I felt something ominous about this request. *Why would the executive general counsel want to call such a meeting?* I fretted.

As the conference call began, the senior vice president of the lender opened with an apology. "We're sorry," he said, "for being the bearers of bad news. We have always worked in good faith with VCS, but our executive general counsel did not approve the funding for this loan. I want you to know this is not how we ordinarily do business. As a senior vice president, I approved the loan, and our bond counsel approved the loan but our executive general counsel would not. I can assure you that I am very disappointed."

A long pause ensued. Not one person on the conference call spoke a word. Finally, Josh Cooperman found his voice.

"This is unacceptable," he said. "Nothing has changed on this side of the ledger. You already had approval of your legal counsel. If you had a legal problem, it should have been discovered before you signed and delivered your term sheet two months ago, committing to fund this loan. What is the basis for such a reversal in your position from then until now?"

One of the lawyers responded, "Because it's the first tax-exempt funding of such a school, this is a very risky investment. Our company is not one to take such risks."

Steve Taber, the municipal bond counsel representing VCS, described the Supreme Court's decision that opened the door for this kind of non-profit funding. He continued, "You can be certain that the bond counsel and I have exhaustively reviewed all these matters in great detail. I am personally signing the opinion letter, backed by Hansen Bridgett, affirming that Valley Christian Schools is indeed legally entitled to receive this tax-exempt bond funding."

WAITING, WAITING . . .

The debate continued for at least ninety minutes. The representatives from the lender would not budge from their position.

Chuck Reed, general legal counsel for Valley Christian Schools, had not spoken. I knew he was listening intently, and I hoped that when the time was right his carefully chosen words would carry considerable weight.

Although introduced at the beginning of the meeting, he identified himself when he broke into the discussion. "I'm Chuck Reed, general legal counsel for the school, and I'm a litigation attorney," he said. "I've been listening to this conversation, and I'm wondering if you've heard of the phrase 'detrimental reliance'? It is questionable whether your company would face a court battle about any First Amendment issues concerning this funding. But it is certain that you will face litigation on the basis of detrimental reliance if your firm fails to fund this bond issue."

After a moment, the senior vice president of the municipal bond division responded that they would need to consult with their corporate board and review their decision. He promised to study the matter and return a phone call within a few days.

While we waited, the meaning of Isaiah 40:31 came into clearer focus: " . . . those who wait on the Lord shall

renew their strength." At the Monday night prayer meeting, I told the intercessors, "It is evident that when multitudes of souls are weighing in the balance, the enemy
will fight at every turn to stop a project like ours. If we
depend only on our own strength, we will fail, because the
enemy's strength is greater than ours. We must call upon
the Lord for His strength if we are to prevail. Let's not be
among those of whom the Scripture warns, 'You have not
because you ask not'" (James 4:2). Fervent prayer continued.

"Wait Upon the Lord"

Since only God can do His work, "wait on
the Lord" to do it. You cannot force progress
even if you try. Position yourself for God to act,
then watch and wait expectantly for what God
will do. Allow time for God to do His work in
His way. Allow Him to teach you through trials
and challenges. Wait, but do not give up on the
vision. God often gives progressive disclosure
to His vision. It seems that the larger the vision,
the longer the lead-time between seeing the
vision and doing the vision. The lead-time
allows adequate prayer, personal spiritual
growth and planning. We were led to purchase
the land for Valley Christian Schools ten years
before God opened the door for city approvals
and for construction to begin. It seemed that the
Skyway campus vision was dead and buried.
But just about the time I was beginning to
question whether I had misunderstood God's
vision, God powerfully resurrected the project.
I have discovered that God allows all to appear
lost just before He shows up and does his

con't.

miraculous work. I call them Cliff hangers! It is a great reminder that He is God and He uses these circumstances to grow our faith.

Forget Plan B

Insist on going forward according to God's "A Team" plans. When obstacles or setbacks arise, pray and ask God to show you how He wants to deal with the situation. Believe that He does not want to settle for Plan B. Do not succumb to fear. God's vision is never lacking His provision. Be open to creative and unprecedented solutions. Remember, "Plans made in heaven are never ten feet too short!"

Chapter 22:12 & 13

Three days after the conference call, we had not heard back from the senior vice president. There was no "Plan B." If the lender failed to fund the tax-exempt issue, the best conventional loan that we could get would leave us at least $11 million short of building the school—and VCS already owed close to $10 million for work in progress.

Five days passed—still no response. Claude Fletcher and I put in a call to the lender, but a vice president explained simply that the issue was still under review.

Another week went by without word. Claude and I rehearsed every possible scenario with Ray Wans, our CFO, and concluded that nothing more could be done except to pray.

Two weeks after the conference call, the senior vice president of the lender phoned. My heart pounded as I heard the verdict.

"Our executive board set aside our executive general counsel on this issue," he said, "and we went to an outside bond counsel. We asked the firm to evaluate Hansen Bridgett's opinion and the tax-exempt funding in regard to the First Amendment issue. Their opinion, I'm pleased to report, is that we can do the deal."

When I could breathe again, I expressed my joy. But what I wanted to do was shout "Praise the Lord!" No wonder the Israelites burst into song when they saw God's great victory after crossing the Red Sea.

On November 1, 1998, I signed my name on more than 300 loan documents. By mid-December, Valley Christian Schools received the net proceeds of the $28 million bond issue into its building trust account. Contractor Rich Furtado and South Bay Construction got paid. Once again, God proved His ability to "supply all . . . needs according to His riches in glory by Christ Jesus" (Philippians 4:19).

Yet many miles remained in our journey to the "promised land" of a new Skyway campus. The biggest pending issue concerned the pool designed to double as a fire-fighting reservoir. Weeks after VCS submitted the engineers' ingenious solution for approval, the San Jose Fire Department still had not responded to the proposed plan. What, I wondered, did this silence mean?

CHAPTER 13
WILL IT FLOAT?

It all seemed so logical. The innovative engineering plans submitted to the San Jose Fire Department in October 1998 for a swimming pool that doubled as a water reservoir would serve several purposes. The design provided a magnificent facility for the aquatic community; it satisfied fire-fighting needs on the hill while avoiding a hideously huge, 200-foot-high water tower; and it was less expensive than building a water tower. Valley Christian Schools awaited what we hoped would be a common-sense decision to approve the design. But all too often we had seen unanticipated obstacles arise in the pursuit of the Skyway campus vision.

The Christmas season of 1998 brought tragic news to the local media headlines. Six people in the San Jose area had died in Christmas tree fires. A heightened awareness spread throughout the community of the risk of death by fire. It was not a good time to be seeking the go-ahead for a new and "unproven" fire safety system.

The holiday season was still underway when we got word that the fire captains had unanimously rejected the plan to use a pool rather than a water tower as a reservoir for fighting fires.

Chancellor Claude Fletcher and I took in this devastating news. "We're back where we started," Claude said. "The city won't allow a giant water tower, and the fire department won't allow a pool as a water reservoir. As it stands now, we can't comply with the fire department's requirements to open school."

"What can we do? Where can we appeal?" I asked. "We must have a solution or we don't have a school!

We're now several months and millions of dollars into excavation, and without a resolution to this dilemma we'll never get a foundation poured."

"We do have a right to make an appeal," Claude responded, "but I found out it's to the same group of fire captains. Also, our appeal must be in writing. They don't allow guests or presentations to the group."

BANGING AT THE DOOR

We knew we had no choice but to exhaust every possible remedy, no matter how unlikely. Claude quickly prepared an appeal and submitted it, while the Monday night prayer group made this matter a priority in persistent intercession to God. We felt as though we were living one of the parables Jesus told during His teaching on prayer, about the man who went to his neighbor begging bread for a guest and would not take no for an answer. He kept banging at the door, despite the midnight hour, until his neighbor got up and gave him what he needed (Luke 11:5–8).

Within days, we received news about our appeal. Our spirits sank—another veto. In a phone call, a representative of the captains' committee said, "What did you expect? They were the same people looking at the same plan. If you can find even one pool that works like your proposed pool, they'll reconsider. There must be some reason why no one else has done this. We're very concerned about life and safety, and the captains won't take a chance on an unproven system."

While distressed by this double denial, we saw a glimmer of hope in the invitation to cite a precedent. Coach Bob Colyar and other "pool parents" began an exhaustive search for a similar system. A couple of weeks later, however, they still had not come up with even one pool that the fire department would accept.

GOD GIVES THE WORD

Despite all evidence to the contrary, I maintained a strong sense that God had already said "yes" to this pool, even though the fire department's answer was "no." During the search for a pool precedent, I was praying and reflecting on this seeming conflict between faith and fact, when a powerful impression came to my mind: *Ask them, "Who in America speaks and every fire chief in America listens?"*

The idea seemed a bit strange. Yet my tenacious feeling that the question should be asked compelled me to pursue it. In response to this inquiry, we were given the name of an engineering firm with such a strong and impeccable reputation that "every fire chief in America would listen." We forwarded our plans immediately.

The firm's analysis was positive. Their report indicated they considered our plans innovative and impressive. They added their engineering approval in the form of a letter dated January 11, 1999, and our hopes were encouraged.

Armed with this confirming validation, Claude Fletcher made a couple of strategic calls and requested a third review that would include the fire chief. The account that followed this meeting made my jaw drop.

After studying the engineering firm's report, the captains gave a unanimous opinion—yet another rejection. In their minds nothing had changed. It was still the same plan.

Then the unbelievable occurred. In the aftermath of this analysis, the fire chief made an executive decision and reversed the ruling. Before the meeting's end, on Tuesday, January 19, 1999, the water tower had become a pool.

My sense of relief was beyond description as I again reflected with awe on Proverbs 21:1, "The king's heart is in the hand of the Lord, like the rivers of water; He turns it wherever He wishes." One thing was certain: Valley's water problem was solved, and these dramatic events transformed a 200-foot water tower into a fifty-three-meter pool.

AN ARK OF A BUILDING

Something else happened during the winter of 1999 that left us in awe of God's plans and purposes. In a unique way He reaffirmed the validity of our Quest for Excellence™ motto, Excellence Brings Influence™.

A few days before the beginning of each school year the VCS faculty and staff gather to focus on God's Word and hear a message from the President/Superintendent. During the past two years I had incorporated into my keynote address a theme describing our students as a "remnant."

My messages included a spotlight on Isaiah 1:9, "Unless the Lord of hosts had left to us a very small remnant, we would have become like Sodom, we would have been made like Gomorrah." The Apostle Paul quotes this verse from Isaiah, and I was impressed that in place of the word "remnant" he uses the word "seed" (Romans 9:29).

"The idea," I explained to the faculty and staff, "is that the 'remnant' is the seed the farmer sets aside from the harvest for the planting of the next harvest. God founded Valley Christian Schools to prepare our students as seed to plant the next great spiritual harvest."

During February 1999, Genia Ferreira, my executive assistant, was hosting an administrator visiting from another school. As we talked about plans for the Skyway campus, Genia drew a picture of the Education Building to illustrate its shape. She glanced at her drawing later and commented, "It looks like Noah's ark!" No one realized then how insightful her comment was.

Soon afterward I was making website updates about the Skyway project for our VCS families. I described the planned Education Building as 450 feet long, or "one and one half times the length of a football field." Later that evening before going to sleep, I remembered that I had given the same "one and one half times the length of a football field" illustration for the length of Noah's ark when I taught Bible to fourth grade students. In a flash I realized the Education Building was the same length as Noah's ark.

What a coincidence, I thought. Then I began to ponder, *Is it really a coincidence?*

GOD CONFIRMS THE
REDEMPTIVE REMNANT

Curiosity about the ark's other dimensions sent me to the description of the ark in Genesis. I wondered, *How high was Noah's ark?* I knew the Education Building was to be forty-five feet tall at its highest point because the City of San Jose had imposed a forty-five-foot height restriction.

I paged back in my Bible to Genesis 6:15 where I discovered—sure enough—the ark was thirty cubits, or forty-five feet tall (a cubit being a foot and a half). In the same verse I noted the ark's width as fifty cubits, or seventy-five feet. But I didn't know the planned width of the Education Building.

During my next meeting with Paul Bunton, the architect, I asked him, "How wide is the Education Building?"

"If you want to know exactly to the foot, I'll have to check," he answered.

Paul unrolled the plans and laid them on a large conference table. He moved his scale back and forth on the blueprints and said, "Right here, it's seventy-five feet."

Grinning, I asked him, "Do you know what that means?"

"What?"

"This building is the same size as Noah's ark!"

"Really?" Paul exclaimed.

"It's true. The dimensions of the ark are given in the Bible, and I've already checked the height and length. Now you've confirmed the width. In each dimension— the length, height, and width—there's an exact match between the ark and the Education Building."

"This really amazes me," I went on. "It seems too improbable to be a coincidence. For the last couple of years I felt God directing me to emphasize to our faculty and staff that our students are a remnant intended to bring a redemptive influence to the world. The righteous remnant in Noah's ark was saved to plant a new generation of humanity that would spread everywhere. I think God must be underscoring the message that He plans to use our students to bring His love, joy, and peace to people around the globe."

Later our top math students accepted the challenge of calculating the probability that the Education Building was "accidentally" planned with the same dimensions as Noah's ark.

Jonathan Burton, a Stanford University alumnus and chair of the VCS science department, sent his students to me to report their calculations. Senior Micah Boersma, soon to become a West Point Cadet, emphatically stated, "With the known variables and various methods of calculation, we came up with odds that are no less than about two million to one. What this means, Dr. Daugherty, is that the dimensions are not an accident. 'Somebody' planned the Education Building to be the same size as Noah's ark." *"Well,"* I reflected, *"it certainly wasn't our architects."*

CHAPTER 14
EXPERIENCING THE VISION

When I saw the first steel beams reaching for the sky at the top of our hill, my heart seemed to reach for the sky with them. There was no turning back now. More than ten years after purchasing the Skyway property, Valley Christian Schools was at last going to have a permanent home. Vision was quickly becoming reality.

Before our contractors poured the foundations of the two main educational buildings, a group of students, parents, and others from the VCS community gathered to place Bibles where the corners of the buildings would stand.

This act signified that Valley Christian Schools' Skyway Campus rested on the foundation of God's Word. The visible construction reminded me that the school, literally and spiritually, is built on the Rock. When I recalled all the miracles God had performed to handle one obstacle to construction after another, my unshakable confidence swelled that the Lord had special plans and purposes in mind for the students who would study here—world-transforming plans.

Think Big

Expect that any vision from God is bigger than any dream you could ever imagine. Depend on God's resources rather than just what you have on hand or in view. If you can easily accomplish a vision yourself, it is probably not of God.

Chapter 22:7

As I looked at the calendar, however, I could see that our desired September 1999 move-in date would have to wait a bit. The delays surrounding approval of the pool design and other issues had pushed our already tight construction schedule past its limit. We had already made contingency arrangements for our students to eke out a few more months at their current locations.

The two churches hosting the junior high students gave permission to remain at their sites, although the teachers faced a challenging situation: They had to pack everything away nightly because the churches used those rooms in the evenings. The high school students had already squeezed into modular buildings on the backside of the Branham campus during the school district's renovation. They were allowed to extend their stay while public school freshmen and sophomores moved in that fall.

When part of the Skyway campus was approved for occupancy, we couldn't let our students wait a moment longer. The gymnasium building was completed first, and in early January 2000, almost 450 junior high school students claimed the new campus as their own. A month later, with the Education Building ready, nearly 1,000 high school students also made it their home. Our move onto the Skyway campus came forty years after Dave and Edie Wallace first opened Valley Christian Schools in 1960.

I marched around the campus taking photos of students walking onto the grounds and through the halls for the first time. I could smell the fresh air at 335 feet above the valley. The freshly mown grass spoke of new beginnings.

In those first days on campus, the launch of "Build the Dream, Experience the Vision"—Valley Christian Schools' first Skyway capital campaign—seemed like a distant memory from another life. Now, with the campus in use, I realized that "Build the Dream" had become "Experience the Vision" for the first time since I had initially walked that barren land in 1988. Everyone I talked with was in awe of what God was doing.

IN A JAM

I was so thrilled to see our long-time dream come true that I considered it an adventure every day to discover and deal with all the little kinks that still needed smoothing out. Moreover, construction of the football stadium and planning for the baseball stadium were still underway when the students moved in. As I would soon learn, the complications of finishing the campus with classes in session presented unique challenges.

My initial euphoria was rudely disturbed by the sounds of big-rig trucks, laden with construction materials, and honking horns. Parents and students had to fight a battle with the heavy equipment to get up the hill on the school's only access road. The Skyway Drive entrance approaches from the south, curves left, and then takes a hairpin turn to the east as it banks up the slope on its way to the crest of the hill. The exit battle to escape at the end of the day was just as bad as the gridlock each morning.

Parents were stuck in their cars for up to forty-five minutes trying to get on and off campus during the morning drop-off of their students and during the afternoon pick-up. This nightmare scenario scared me. Some parents asked, "What kind of planning went into this place? I can't be forty-five minutes late to work every day!" Traffic jams of vehicles coming onto the campus backed up for more than a third of a mile with stop-and-go traffic.

I contacted Gerry DeYoung of Ruth and Going, our engineering firm, for help with the traffic jams. He suggested a modification of the traffic loop, but also explained that congestion would remain a challenge until construction of the campus was completed. The worst day came before seven o'clock one morning when a big truck pulling a loaded flatbed trailer stalled just past the hairpin turn. No one could get on or off campus until after 9 a.m.

As traffic lessons were learned and construction subsided, the amazement and awe of driving onto the beautiful hilltop campus gradually returned. The splendor of God's handiwork was a constant reminder of His ongoing guidance and blessings.

FIND A NEED AND FILL IT

The Skyway site remained a work in progress. Shortly after our students moved in, I began to explore the west side of the property for a solution to a lingering problem.

Back in the fall of 1998, not long after South Bay Construction began grading the site, a new possibility for flat space had become apparent. In the engineers' original design, the area inside the hairpin turn was to become a hill by relocating excess dirt and rock. But as I watched the earthmoving begin I saw that the land inside the turn could become a level pad. I called a halt to the hill building and contacted Gerry DeYoung. After some discussion, the engineers at Ruth and Going agreed to design a flat space instead of a steep hill.

This decision added a plot of treasured land, but left a problem on our hands. The 30,000 cubic yards of dirt and rock no longer forming the hill needed a new home. Simply hauling this load away would carry a price tag of about $500,000. Moreover, finding a suitable off-site location proved challenging because of the naturally occurring asbestos in the serpentine rock. The asbestos content caused the dirt and rock to be classified as hazardous waste. As consultants mulled over what to do, heavy equipment moved the excess dirt to the east side of the Skyway property where the pile was kept watered to eliminate dust.

Just after we began moving onto the campus in January of 2000, I drove to the parking lot used by our high school seniors and examined the area on the southwest side of our property. I sensed God wanted us to understand something more about our circumstances.

My eyes fixed on a large gully just south of Tom DeHart's home and west of the senior parking lot. I remembered Tom as the helpful neighbor who had sold us the triangle of land we needed to complete the full-size baseball field and the fifty-three-meter pool.

"That gully could take all of our excess dirt and become flat land," I reflected. *"I wonder if it belongs to the DeHarts?"*

As it turned out, the gully did belong to Tom, and he was willing to help again. In exchange for his gully, the school agreed to create a building pad on part of the newly leveled ground next to his home and to provide a sewer connection into Valley's main line. No money changed hands. By that summer, earthmovers filled the gully with all our excess dirt and rock, and left us a wonderful new flat area.

I commented to our building committee, "It looks like we've discovered another plan from the drawing board of heaven."

DEALING WITH "CAN WE AFFORD IT?"

More challenges arose in those early months of 2000 as we pushed ahead to complete the campus. While the football stadium was under construction, the architect for the baseball stadium, John Milburn, tried furiously to finish his plans and get approvals from the City of San Jose. I was determined to get another classroom or two into the design of the baseball stadium, but tension about the scope and cost of the stadium resonated in meeting after meeting. "We need the education space," I explained. "Demand has already exceeded capacity, and more classroom space is crucial. I thought we all had agreed on this."

The day came when plans for the proposed baseball stadium arrived for my approval. Although I had turned more of my daily attention back to educational development, I was anxious to see the stadium plans. The meeting convened in the boardroom, where I inspected drawings displayed around the room. As John Milburn began his presentation, he reviewed the priorities of being on schedule and on budget. He didn't get far into his talk before it became obvious that those two priorities did not allow for another classroom.

A sick feeling surged in my gut. Something compelled me to make certain that at least one classroom was included. I explained my disappointment, and John explained why the priorities precluded an added classroom. Still, I couldn't get comfortable with this loss, and expressed emphatic regret.

Our CFO, Ray Wans, spoke up with distress in his voice. "Cliff, this is a baseball stadium, not an education building, and we've got to control costs. Our donors did not anticipate the cost of a classroom. What will they think?"

Someone else added, "We can't afford more delays. Every delay costs more money."

"How much time and money are we talking about?" I asked.

John Milburn pondered the question. "It would put

us another two weeks behind and cost somewhere around another $300,000 to add a classroom in the stadium. And it won't be easy. I'm already struggling to meet the construction schedule and the budget. Going back to the city with revisions is never painless. I want to do what you want, but I'm getting mixed messages. Something has to give."

The pressure to move forward and live within the budget was intense. I found myself praying silently. *Is it You who is prompting me to be so determined, Lord? Or is it just a bullheaded Cliff that won't give up on the idea to find another classroom?*

A sudden thought came to my mind and I popped a question to our CFO.

"Ray, I know you are doing your job to keep costs under control. What is the annual revenue on thirty added students?"

We both did some mental math. I rounded off thirty times, say, $10,000 per student in tuition. After the calculation, I was startled by the $300,000 figure—a number that represented increased income each year.

Instantly, everyone in the room seemed to realize that even the bottom line demanded an added classroom. The pressurized emotional tone in the room abated and the discussion turned to how to move the plans forward with a classroom in the stadium. My burdened lifted. The answer was clear: We couldn't afford not to add a classroom.

Thank You, Lord!

Later the Lord surprised us with yet another remarkable turn of events. He prompted VCS supporters to cover the entire cost of the stadium, including the classroom.

Will we never learn, I wondered, *to stop allowing worries about cost to determine our decisions?* Perhaps no one ever gets past this issue entirely, but I am learning to check myself before asking the "but can we afford it?" question. The first and most important question should be, "Does God want it?" After so many of God's awesome provisions, I'm getting the idea that the Lord is not short on cash, and His vision is never lacking His provision.

CHAPTER 15
THE TRUE MEASURE OF SUCCESS

The administrative offices buzzed with anticipation as Valley Christian Schools prepared for our formal dedication of the Skyway campus in May 2000. Although various development projects remained pending, we were eager to host a celebration of all God had accomplished in making the Skyway campus a reality.[2]

As plans for the ceremony went forward on our beautiful new site, however, I became aware of an undercurrent of unhappiness among the VCS teachers about funding priorities. Although we had made efforts over the years to raise faculty salaries, including establishing the $1 million Teacher Endowment Fund, VCS teachers were still paid poorly compared to public school teachers. For the sake of the school's ministry, faculty members had always accepted relatively low salaries with the understanding that the administration and VCS board provided all they could with the available resources.

But after moving onto the Skyway property, teachers saw that God was providing millions of dollars for building the campus, prompting both gratitude and puzzlement. During the eighteen-month period before and during construction, the Lord spoke to donors to provide a phenomenal outpouring of more than $30 million in cash and stocks for completion of the Skyway campus. Amid some of the finest instructional, performing arts, and athletic facilities among secondary schools in America, the teachers began to question how they were valued compared to the new facilities.

"We were willing to sacrifice for the ministry

when money was scarce," they told me. "But things have changed. Now tens of millions of dollars are spent here. It seems that buildings are more important than teachers, because all of the money is going toward the facilities."

JUGGLING POTS ON
A FOUR-BURNER STOVE

I joined the faculty meetings and listened to the teachers' concerns. Their plight pained me, especially because the excellence of our faculty had soared over the years. As I responded I compared the situation to cooking on a four-burner kitchen stove.

"Valley Christian Schools is serving a four-course meal of quality Christian education to our students," I explained in my analogy. "There are four pots on this four-burner stove: improved teacher salaries in the Teacher Endowment pot, new school facilities in the Capital Fund pot, quality materials and equipment in the Instructional pot, and tuition assistance funds in the Youth With Promise[TM3] pot. Although the Teacher Endowment Fund has been on a back burner since 1998, it's still on the stove. We want a balanced meal of Christian education, but we can stir only one pot at a time. We have to stir the facilities pot till it's 'done' to secure a place for teachers to teach and for students to learn. As soon as facilities are secured, we'll move the Teacher Endowment pot back to the front burner."

The teachers appeared somber as they listened to my explanation. I knew many of them did not have enough money to stop by McDonald's on the way home, and their feedback later told me that all this talk about pots on a stove did not help.

Rumblings continued. "Dr. Daugherty's intentions are good," some teachers reasoned, "but it will probably take years before a change in priorities will make any real difference in our salaries."

I continued our conversations; confident the teachers would understand why substantial increased salaries were not possible at this time. I described the situation as similar to a young family buying their first home, when the expenses just keep coming. First there's the down payment, then moving costs, then the first monthly mortgage bill. Before long, Mom runs to Dad in a panic, asking, "What happened to the food money? I need to buy groceries!" I tried to explain that our school was facing the same kind of "new home" financial challenges. Yet the teachers, stretching their own frugal household budgets, remained disappointed.

NOT JUST DEDICATION—
CONSECRATION

This unresolved issue remained in my mind as the school prepared for our two weeks of dedication and commitment for our new facilities. On Monday, May 8, after a service in the large gym, more than 1,700 students, faculty, and staff gathered on the sidewalks that bordered the grassy commons. As we surrounded the flags flying there, we symbolically encircled the campus in prayer. We prayed that Valley Christian Schools would remain loyal to God's purposes for succeeding generations.

At the public dedication on Sunday, May 21, Dr. Mike Beever, by then chair of the VCS board of directors, gave a stirring message about God's plans and purposes for Valley Christian Schools. He reminded all of us that we were assembled not just to dedicate facilities but to consecrate—set aside for a high and holy purpose—the entire campus, the ministry, and all those who serve and learn at Valley Christian Skyway Campus.

Mike captured my thoughts and feelings when he said, "All of us who have worked on the Skyway project were taken to another dimension of God's care. It seemed as though we were caught up in something so much greater than any of us had imagined. Events moved forward at warp speed. There was the feeling that we were like a small child running to keep step with his Father, and then to know the incredible experience of being caught up into our Father's arms and carried by Him through the completion of the project. He is so clearly in control; we have just had the joy and thrill of coming along for the ride."

After the ceremony in the air-conditioned gym, people streamed out into the blazing sunshine. Many stopped at the entry to the plaza to look at the pair of granite stones placed into the walkway during construction. These five-foot stone diamonds, called the Alpha and Omega stones, were inscribed with the first verse of Genesis and verses from the last chapter of Revelation. People prayed that these stones, revealing God's Word, would speak life to all those who entered the campus and serve as a reminder that the Bible is always at the heart of Valley Christian Schools.

We mounted a bronze plaque in the lobby of the high school to honor David and Edie Wallace, founders of Valley Christian Schools forty years earlier, who attended the ceremony. The plaque highlighted their founding purpose: "That the students might know that in Christ are hidden all the treasures of wisdom and knowledge . . . so that whatsoever they do in word or in deed will be done in the name of the Lord Jesus, giving thanks to God and the Father by Him (Col. 2:3, 3:17)."

WHAT WILL IT TAKE?

At home after the dedication, my thoughts returned to the teachers and my ongoing dialog with God about their salaries. Like the teachers, I began to question Him. "God, if You can speak to people to contribute $30 million in such a short time to build the campus, why can't You do something to meet the needs of our teachers?"

Duke It Out

Give yourself permission to wrestle with your doubts, and to work through the "why" questions. Ask God to help you understand scriptural truths that apply to your situation. Ask God for the faith to make a wholehearted commitment to move forward in the face of unanswered questions like, "Where will we get the money?"

Chapter 22: 16

I tried to calculate what kind of endowment would allow VCS to increase each teacher's pay by about $1,000 per month. With approximately 110 teachers, I figured we would need just over $1 million of interest income each year.[4] At then-current interest rates I guessed it might take an endowment of at least $15–17 million to give our teachers that kind of a raise. Since that was about the size of our budget for the 1999–2000 school year, it seemed like an overwhelming challenge.

I remembered how our first Teacher Endowment Fund drive required ten years to raise $1 million. At that pace it could take up to 170 years to establish an adequate endowment. *Hmm,* I reflected. *That's another impossible dream, apart from God.*

The numbers appeared too daunting. But as I continued to pray, I heard questions arise from my spirit: *Doesn't God care for our teachers as much as He cares about building a place for teachers to teach and students to learn? Is it my faith that is lacking?*

> **Maintain an Exceptionally Qualified and Properly Compensated Executive Leadership Team, Faculty, and Staff.**
>
> Chapter 18: 4

Suddenly I felt my confidence swell. I remembered the truth from James 4:2: "You do not have because you do not ask." I decided to ask, and I discovered my heart sincerely asking God for an extra $1 million per year for teachers' salaries.

Excitement rose as I sensed the Lord speaking to me: *"I do care about the teachers, and I am able to provide,"* He seemed to say. *"And further, I will! Just wait and see!"*

THE STAIRS

As I pondered, a sudden directive struck my thoughts. *Tell everyone that until God meets our teachers' needs, we will not tile the steps on the cement stairways in the buildings. Teachers are more important to God than installing tile on the stairs.*

Absolutely! my spirit shouted in response. *Yes, that's true!*

At that point, we had a list of about $2.2 million worth of unfinished items that we needed to complete. The installation of tile on the stairs appeared on the list with an estimated cost of $70,000.

> **No Secrets**
> Always share the vision that God gives to you with those who will listen. On more than one occasion I have shared God's vision with people of seemingly modest means that eventually gave tens of thousands or millions of dollars in response to God's leading. Be faithful to share the vision but understand that it is only God who can lead people to give their time, talent and treasure from their hearts.
> Chapter 22: 18

At the beginning of June I began telling this message to anyone who would listen: "Until God meets our teacher's needs, we will not tile the stairs." Every day on campus, walking the cement stairs became a "prayer walk" as we remembered the need for better faculty salaries. If the Lord intended to raise the needed funds through special donations, I could only trust that He would speak to those He wanted to give.

Only a few days after I started sharing the message of the stairs, God confirmed His intentions. On my way home the next week I stopped by an aquatics competition at the pool and shared the story of the stairs. One person there, clearly moved by the Holy Spirit, responded with an astounding affirmation.

"I agree!" the individual said. "Go ahead and announce to the teachers that they will receive no less than an additional $1 million each year for at least the next ten years."

My heart leaped at this pledge that exactly matched what I had asked of God. It seemed unreal. I later reflected on the words of Jesus to the two blind men: "'Do you believe that I am able to do this?' They said to Him, 'Yes,

Lord.' Then he touched their eyes, saying, 'It shall be done to you according to your faith'" (Matthew 9:28–29, NAS).

Before the end of the month VCS received the initial payment of this pledge, and by September teachers started drawing extra pay from the first million-dollar gift during the 2000–2001 school year. During the ten years of this annual million-dollar commitment, the school is setting aside funds to enable VCS to continue supporting better faculty salaries for decades to come.[5]

Through this amazing answer to specific prayer, God more than proved how much He does care for our teachers and is able and willing to meet their needs with loving generosity.

GOD'S VISION NEVER
LACKS HIS PROVISION

The long saga of how God provided a permanent home for the high school and junior high does not encompass all He has done for Valley Christian Schools. Our elementary school has walked through its own adventure story.

During 2000, we learned that the by the end of the 2000–2001 academic year VCS would lose our long-time lease of the Howes Elementary campus. The Howes campus housed Valley's 450 kindergarten through fifth-grade students. Our executive team scrambled to find a new location for the next year, but again options were scarce.

Meanwhile, Ray Wans, the VCS chief financial officer, knew that Trinity Lutheran Church, his home congregation in San Jose, had some extra land where a school might be built. Ray approached Trinity with a proposal to lease land from the church for VCS to build a school. From the start, the project faced logistical challenges as well as opposition from nearby residents who feared how the project might disturb their neighborhood. The clock ticked on during months of negotiation and prayer. When fall 2001 arrived, Valley's kindergarten through fifth-graders became temporarily homeless and had to take up transitional housing at two churches in the area.

Finally, the city, school, and community reached a compromise on the campus layout. The San Jose City Council unanimously approved the building plans on January 22, 2002, and VCS broke ground February 24.

Again, before our contractors poured the foundations of the Leigh Campus, a group of students and parents placed Bibles in the foundation where the corners of the building would stand. As before, his act signified that Valley Christian Schools' Leigh Campus rested on the foundation of God's Word and that the school, literally and spiritually, is built on the Rock.

More hurdles lay ahead. Planning delays and a fire that destroyed about one-third of the new building interrupted construction and added $1.8 million to the project. We launched another urgent capital campaign to raise the final payment to the builders. The VCS community rallied around the theme, "Delayed but not denied." The theme verse was Jeremiah 29:11.

By February 2003 the new campus at 1450 Leigh Avenue in San Jose received its first pupils. The 30,000 square-foot, two-story school boasts twenty-two media-rich classrooms with high-speed Internet access, a library, an instrumental music room and a large playground. For the first time in more than forty years since the school opened in 1960, all Valley Christian School students had their own permanent facilities. What a gift of stability!

God's goodness was on my mind one morning as I walked to my office, greeting students and staff

and enjoying the magnificent Skyway campus. A grateful swell of appreciation arose once again for the many
ways God has worked wonders to accomplish His will
for Valley Christian Schools. Over and over I experienced
a timeless truth, that God's vision never lacks His provision. I learned that God's vision is larger than our dreams
and that plans should always be sized to His vision and
not what we think we can afford. God never fails to fund
his vision when we allow His work to be accomplished
through our obedience.

Think Big

Expect that any vision from God is bigger
than any dream you could ever imagine. Depend
on God's resources rather than just what you
have on hand or in view. If you can easily
accomplish a vision yourself, it is probably not
of God.

Chapter 22: 7

Near the entrance to the Education Building I
paused to glance again at a bronze plaque posted on the
wall about a month before the campus dedication. Head-
lined "Arise and Build," it features the written prayer I
took to the VCS board of directors on January 8, 1998,
recounting God's miraculous provision of both faith and
resources throughout Valley's history. The plaque com-
memorates the day when our entire board received the gift
of Jesus' faith to build over 200,000 square feet of school
construction valued at more than $100 million by 2006.

Psalm 127:1 testifies, "Unless the Lord builds the
house, they labor in vain who build it." If the Lord plans
to build, however, nothing—*nothing*—can stand in His
way.

"Look among the nations and watch—be utterly astounded! For I will work a work in your days which you would not believe, though it were told you" (Habakkuk 1:5).

CHAPTER 16
"CAN IT WORK FOR ME?"

As I looked back on my years with Valley Christian Schools I reflected on its amazing transformation from a sinking ship into the USS Valley Christian, a beautiful, ocean-going luxury liner. The transformed USS Valley Christian transports thousands of students toward all that God intends to accomplish through their lives around the world. It is such a privilege to serve on the bridge with Captain Jesus. The view is great and the lifeboats were never needed. In fact the lifeboats were discarded and the added space accommodates even more passengers.

Not long after Valley Christian Schools took occupancy of the Skyway campus, I spent some time one morning pondering our need for additional funds to complete the facilities. During my reflection and prayer, a passage came alive to me from the second chapter of Haggai. I could clearly hear God's voice speaking to me, to our VCS board of directors, and to our administrative team as I read and reread this chapter.

God's message was so unmistakable that I found myself quoting from the chapter at our Tuesday morning administrative team meeting of about fourteen VCS principals, administrators, and support staff. My heart burned with passion as I delivered the devotion for the meeting.

I read: "Speak now to . . . all the remnant of the people, and say, 'Who is left among you that saw this house in its former glory? How do you see it now? Is it not in your sight as nothing?'" (Haggai 2:2, RSV).

• God has shown us that our students are the remnant—the seed from the previous harvest that the farmer puts into the barn for the planting of the next great spiritual harvest. God confirmed that truth strongly to us in the discovery of the "ark" in the dimensions of the Education Building. (See Isaiah 1:9 and Romans 9:29, where the words used are "remnant" and "seed" in the King James and in the New King James Versions.)

• Remember how we wanted to purchase the Branham campus? We made offers to buy it but they were rejected because God had a better plan. Here we are sitting in a beautiful conference room that overlooks the San Jose city skyline and the distant hills! How good God is to us. Our past campus provisions now seems as "nothing" compared to our new Skyway campus.

While giving the devotion during the administrative team meeting, I continued reading the next verses from Haggai 2. "Yet now take courage . . . work, for I am with you, says the Lord of hosts, according to the promise that I made you when you came out of Egypt. My Spirit abides among you; fear not. For thus says the Lord of hosts: Once again, in a little while, I will shake the heavens and the earth and the sea and the dry land; and I will shake all nations, so that the treasures of all nations shall come in, and I will fill this house with splendor, says the Lord of hosts. The silver is mine, and the gold is mine, says the Lord of hosts. The latter splendor of this house shall be greater than the former, says the Lord of hosts; and in this place I will give prosperity, says the Lord of hosts" (Haggai 2:4–9, RSV).

• From these verses I sense God telling us to go forward in faith to complete the school with confident assurance. This passage gives me confidence that God will faithfully prosper the development of His great work at Valley Christian Schools in ways we cannot even imagine.

Getting back to the passage I read, "Pray now, consider what will come to pass from this day onward. Before a stone was placed upon a stone in the temple of the Lord, how did you fare? When one came to a heap of twenty measures, there were but ten; when one came to the wine vat to draw fifty measures, there were but twenty. . . . Since the day that the foundation of the Lord's temple was laid, consider" (Haggai 2:15–18, RSV).

- The message for our school from these verses is that Christian schools often perceive themselves as among the "have-nots" of the educational world. Valley Christian Schools struggled with such an impression of itself at times. It seemed that there was never enough money, equipment, facilities, curriculum, or talented teachers. We had to overcome the misguided view of many that scarcity and a willingness to sacrifice without adequate resources is somehow a measure of spirituality. The mindset that says, "I'd rather sacrifice and do with less than the best in order to have a Christian education," has too often been the rationale for inferior quality, as if prosperity and spirituality are mutually exclusive. How easy it is to lull ourselves into a prideful contentment with our scarcity in the guise of "doing without for the Lord."

- Measuring our spirituality by our means is always wrong. It is just as wrong to imply that wealth is a measure of spirituality as it is to say that scarcity is a measure of spirituality. In God's economy, prosperity has little if anything to do with money. Prosperity in God's economy is a measure of the soul's abundance, and is best measured by faith, hope, love, and the fruit of the Holy Spirit, as affirmed in 1 Corinthians 13:13 and Galatians 5:22–23.

- The message here is clear. Building God's temple requires God's provision. His temple is expensive, but God—not any of us—is the architect, builder, and funding resource for His temple. Building our own temples will leave us reliant on what we can afford rather than on what God will bless us with if we allow Him to do His work, in His way, in His time, through our hands. How privileged are we that God has chosen to use our hands!
- Prayer is the key to unlocking God's provision for the soul and our Christian school ministry. I like the New King James translation of 3 John 2: "Beloved, I pray that you may prosper in all things and be in health, just as your soul prospers."
- Back in Haggai 2 I read, "Is the seed yet in the barn? Do the vine, the fig tree, the pomegranate, and the olive tree still yield nothing? From this day on I will bless you" (Haggai 2:19, RSV).
- The words "From this day on I will bless you" have struck my heart powerfully as being God's message for Valley Christian Schools. It's a new day. God has chosen to reflect His splendor through VCS and His students here. The Quest for Excellence™ at Valley Christian Schools can be nothing more or less than a reflection of the nature, character and works of God.

The final three verses in the passage concluded, " . . . I am about to shake the heavens and the earth, and to overthrow the throne of kingdoms; I am about to destroy the strength of the kingdoms of the nations, and overthrow the chariots and their riders; and the horses and their riders shall go down, every one by the sword of his fellow. On that day says the Lord of hosts, I will take you, O Zerubbabel my servant . . . says the Lord, and make you like a signet ring; for I have chosen you, says the Lord of Hosts" (Haggai 2:21–23, RSV).

- My devotional comments concluded: Many forces among the kingdoms of this world have arrayed themselves against Christian schools that reflect the splendor of God. But God will "overthrow" those forces so that those whom God has chosen to develop quality Christian schools will have the blessings and resources of God to build. These extraordinary Christian schools will train youth as the Lord's ambassadors with a powerful redemptive influence in the world.

Develop the God-given talents of students to achieve their God-intended life's work.

Chapter 20: 5

AFFIRMATIONS OF WIDER MINISTRY

At the next meeting of the VCS board of directors, I shared this same devotional. Then, and many times since, God affirmed this message unmistakably in the hearts of the VCS board members. In fact, they cited the words of Jesus to me, " . . . to whom much is given, from him much will be required . . ." (Luke 12:48). Several shared a strong impression that God was preparing Valley Christian Schools as a prototype or template Christian school for other schools to follow. They told me not to be surprised when God led me to help other school administrators understand how He plans to bless their schools in the same way He has blessed VCS.

This thought stirred my spirit, and I wondered what such an assignment from God might look like. Once again I thanked God for giving Valley Christian Schools such capable, CEO-quality board members to support and direct His work at VCS under the guidance of the Holy Spirit.

Late that summer of 2000, Eduardo Lorenzo, senior pastor of a large church in Adrogué, Argentina, came by my office during a visit to California. I had heard him speak when I visited Argentina with Ed Silvoso in 1992. We had also met at one of the Pastors' Prayer Summits at Mount Hermon Conference Center near Santa Cruz, California. Pastor Lorenzo came to the school with a word he felt God wanted me to know. He explained that the Lord built Valley Christian Schools not only for VCS students but also for students at many other schools whose leaders would be inspired and challenged to build similar facilities.

Hmm, there's that message again! I thought. Reverend Lorenzo was very encouraging, and I expressed my appreciation for his kindness.

Not long afterward, school administrators and even entire boards of other Christian schools began visiting the Skyway campus for ideas and insight on how to build their schools. Several teams made more than one visit. I have enjoyed reciprocal excursions to meet with their boards or parent groups and explain some of the principles and practices God has taught us through our journey. (See Chapter 18 for a summary.)

On Friday, October 11, 2002, Eduardo Lorenzo made a return call to my office. This time Pam Watson, my executive assistant, recorded his message.

In part Pastor Lorenzo said, "God has something on the horizon for you. It is not just about the school or the educational training that is happening here, but it is about something much bigger—something beyond Valley Christian Schools."

A GROWING INFLUENCE
I often wondered what all of this meant. As time went on God continued to bless Valley Christian Schools

in almost all areas. Our 2005–06 budget climbed to about $25 million, growing each year. The value of the facilities God so wondrously provided exceeded $100 million. That school year ended with 1,140 high school students, 540 junior high students, and about 412 elementary pupils at the Leigh Avenue campus. The quality of students continued to improve.

> **Plan Such Exceptional Programs and Specialized Facilities That God Will Attract Extraordinarily Capable People to Help Fund Their Development**
>
> Chapter 18: 3

VCS students gained increasing recognition for achievements in academics, athletics, and many other pursuits including music, dance, and theater. The school, its departments, and individual students won awards and championships at regional, state, and national levels. (See Chapter 21 for specific examples.) We thank God for forming Valley Christian Schools into one of the premier comprehensive college preparatory kindergarten-through-twelfth-grade school programs in the United States.

In October 2004, Valley Christian High School was honored to receive the "No Child Left Behind" Blue Ribbon Award from the U.S. Department of Education. We had applied for Blue Ribbon status at the suggestion of Dr. Joel Torode, VCHS' principal. I thought our chances seemed slim to achieve the award during our first year of making application. Among the myriad of requirements for application, Valley Christian High School had to show evidence that student academic achievement scores ranked among the top ten percent in the nation.

I was amazed and pleased when Valley Christian

High School became the only private high school in California to receive the prestigious Blue Ribbon Award that year. I learned later that only four private high schools in the entire nation had earned the honored Blue Ribbon distinction. Including public schools and K–12 schools, Valley Christian High School was one of just seven high schools in California and forty-one high schools in the country to achieve Blue Ribbon status in 2004.

CONSECRATING A PROTOTYPE

A remarkable sequence of events began in the winter of 2005 that confirmed what God was saying in various ways and through various people about His plans and purposes for VCS. After I went to bed on Tuesday, February 1, 2005, I sensed the presence of the Lord strongly as I picked up my Bible to read. Lying on my back, I thought, *I want to hear something special from the Lord this evening.* I closed my eyes and turned my Bible upside down and around until I was not sure whether the back or front was facing me and which side was up. (I don't recommend this as a common practice!) Before opening my eyes I opened the Bible, and began to read where my eyes landed on the first word. It was 1 Kings 9:1:

"And it came to pass, when Solomon had finished building the house of the Lord and the king's house, and all Solomon's desire which he wanted to do, that the Lord appeared to Solomon the second time, as He had appeared to him at Gibeon. And the Lord said to him: 'I have heard your prayer and your supplication that you have made before Me; I have sanctified this house which you have built to put My name there forever, and My eyes and My heart will be there perpetually.'"

Get A Clue!

Understand that a God-given vision is getting a glimpse of what God wants to do through you. When God gives you a vision, He will give you the faith and the means to see it happen.

Chapter 22:6

I was deeply moved and sensed that God was speaking these words to me personally about Valley Christian Schools. *Could there be a connection with tomorrow morning's meeting?* I wondered. Chancellor Claude Fletcher and I, along with another friend of the school, had invited about forty people to a 7 a.m. capital campaign breakfast at the Capital Club in downtown San Jose. The date was Wednesday, February 2, 2005. I was to speak to the theme "Finishing the Skyway Campus" and the $1.88 million needed for completion. It hit me while reading God's message to Solomon that He was now speaking to me about the Skyway campus.

During my talk at the Capital Club the next morning, I found myself saying, "I believe God will use our school as a prototype to launch about twenty more schools like VCS during my lifetime." I could sense that the forty-some people in attendance resonated with the idea, and that God was affirming, *"Yes, and I'll do it."*

Claude Fletcher then stood and said, "Cliff has been saying this for a while, but I didn't really see it as real until yesterday. A group from Denver, Colorado, flew in to San Jose on a private Learjet to visit VCS with the intent of building a campus like ours. They have all the ingredients needed to do it. I now believe that God is in this and will use VCS as a prototype to build twenty or more quality Christian high schools."

We had spent the whole day with the team from

Colorado, explaining how to allow God to do among them what He has done at VCS. In an e-mail that the team leader sent to me two days later, he wrote, "All of us were so excited by what we saw; we hardly needed an airplane to fly home! . . . What you all have accomplished is awesome: truly excellent. We will certainly keep you posted regarding our progress in Denver."

Expect Confirmation
God sometimes confirms His message through a persistent, deeper sense of "knowing," or He may speak through Scripture reading, or through various circumstances of life. On occasion, He confirms His guidance through other people and often through a combination of means. When you sense that God is speaking, do not be afraid to ask Him for confirmation and correct understanding. . . .

Chapter 22: 9

THE SECOND PHASE—MUCH BIGGER

The confirming words continued. On Saturday, February 5, I woke up at 1:47 a.m., according to the big red numbers on the clock. Again I sensed God's presence in a powerful manner, and I wondered what it meant. I prayed and listened. I looked at the clock again and it read 2:00 a.m. exactly.

Then I heard God say in my thoughts, "Remember, it was February 2, 1998, at the Pastors' Prayer Summit when I spoke to you and told you that I would build the school. You wrote that date in your Bible by the passages I gave you to pass on to the board. When I spoke to you late on Tuesday, February 1, 2005, with the 1 Kings passage, it was exactly seven years later—the last day of a seven-year period. You are working to complete the funding of the Skyway campus this summer. August 20, 2005, will be exactly seven years from first day of construction to the completion of the school. Seven is My perfect number—one week. I have shown this to you so you can know for certain that I have done this work, and that I will achieve my purposes through anyone who will catch a glimpse of what I want to do through their lives and be pleased to let Me work."

The Lord continued, "I have a second phase of work that I will do through you and the team that I am bringing to you. I will move My work of Christian education far beyond San Jose, across the nation and into many other places around the world. It is just as I told you through Eduardo Lorenzo, 'This is big—much bigger than what you have done so far.' The second work is beginning. Ed Silvoso's visit to your office on Thursday, February 3, 2005, with Dave Thompson was not an accident. I sent him. Just as Ed was used by Me to help you in the first phase of this work, I will use him again to help launch the second phase."

About this time my wife stirred from her sleep, and I told Kris all about these thoughts and impressions. We lay quietly in awe and wonder. We agreed that if the Lord was truly speaking, then the date of February 2 for His message at the Pastors' Prayer Summit seven years earlier and the date of the groundbreaking on August 20, 1998, would prove accurate.

The next day I confirmed exact matches for both dates. The dates penned next to passages in my Bible from the Pastors' Prayer Summit read "2–2-98." I wondered how I could confirm the August 20, 1998, date for the groundbreaking. Then I remembered seeing some photos in my desk drawer at home. I found a stack that included some photos from that period. The only ones with dates written on the back were photos of the first bulldozer cutting the ground on the first day of construction. I was amazed to see the date on the back—August 20, 1998! My confidence grew that it really was God who had spoken to me during the night. People who know me understand that I have a hard time remembering the birthdays of even my closest family members. The message no doubt came from the Lord.

MORE CONFIRMATION

Another important confirmation of this message would be whether we successfully raised the needed $1.88 million for the "Finishing the Skyway Campus" capital campaign by the August 20, 2005, date. When I presented the amounts targeted for the campaign at the Capital Club breakfast, we had included $250,000 for resurfacing our all-weather track in the football stadium. In the meantime, we had learned of an all-weather track surface developed by Mondo, a company that boasts the highest quality and the fastest times of all tracks. I discovered that almost all of the world record track times were achieved on a Mondo track surface. Our commitment to excellence demanded that we install the Mondo surface so that Valley Christian Schools could reflect the splendor of God and—as I have sometimes said— "help make God look good to those who don't know Him yet."

For the track program, a world-class Mondo track surface certainly answers the question, "What does your department have to offer that people would say, 'If you want that, you have to go to Valley Christian?'" The problem? I had already announced a $1.88 capital campaign, and the Mondo track appeared to add another $750,000 to the tab. We prayed for God's guidance.

When many of our football parents and several of

our administrators met on the football field on Thursday evening, June 9, 2005, to switch on our new football lights for the first time, I took the opportunity to discuss our Mondo track option. By Wednesday, June 22, the issue was settled. Donor commitments not only exceeded the $1.88 million goal; they topped the $2.63 million mark to completely pay for the Mondo track. All of the funds were committed for receipt by the school by the end of July or the beginning of August—well in advance of the August 20th deadline.

Yes, I concluded, God was continuing to confirm His message in many ways. I was reminded again that "His vision is never lacking His provision" and that "His vision is always bigger than our dreams." Certainly, I saw the truth of God's promise to achieve His purposes through anyone who will catch a glimpse of what He wants to do through their lives and be pleased to let Him work through them. Since early Saturday morning on February 5, 2005, I have become more convinced than ever that the Lord is launching a second phase of work to extend the Excellence Brings Influence™ movement in ways that we cannot yet comprehend.

BEYOND ACADEMICS

I imagined how God might use what He is doing at Valley Christian Schools to inspire and guide others to develop many more Christian high schools. I further imagined how the influence of Valley Christian Schools could even go beyond the academic setting and touch many other endeavors within the marketplace.

The vision took hold to launch a Quest for Excellence Institute. The idea is to promote the principles and practices of the Quest for Excellence™ in every profession of influence. I could see how these principles are transferable to people in any vocation. (See Chapter 19.)

One example of a Christian's influence in the banking profession can be seen in Chuck Ripka. Chuck is an amazing Christian banker who helped found Riverview Community Bank in Otsego, Minnesota. Chuck and I discussed the idea for the Quest Institute for Christian Schools™ when he came to speak in our high school chapel. He described how God is using him to serve the Lord through Riverview Community Bank. After we compared notes, we discovered that our recent journeys—to build the schools and the bank—were very similar. When Chuck heard about the institute, he volunteered to head the seminars for bankers. Other people in varied professions have expressed interest as well.

EXCELLENCE? BY WHOSE STANDARD?

One day Linda Skovmand, Director of Public Relations and Quality Assurance for VCS, brought an independent consulting team into my office. There were smiles all around. The team was excited to show their proposal for a poster and advertisement campaign. When they unveiled the poster, the scent of fresh ink added to the luster of one word emboldened across the top of the board: "EXCELLENCE!"

The team anticipated my approval, but their smiles turned to confusion when they saw the look on my face. The declaration scared me.

"That would be false advertising," I said bluntly. "We can't say that Valley Christian Schools is excellent."

Astonished, the lead presenter asked, "How could this be false advertising? We've checked out VCS, and we've never seen such an excellent school. There is nothing better anywhere. If this school isn't excellent, what school is?"

"It's a question of 'By whose standard?'" I answered. "The Bible teaches, ' . . . But they, measuring themselves by themselves, and comparing themselves among themselves, are not wise,'" I said, quoting 2 Corinthians 10:12.

"The ultimate standard of excellence is the nature, character, and works of God," I continued. "That's why we can't claim to be excellent. We are on a Quest for Excellence. As it says in 1 John 3:2, ' . . . we know that when He is revealed, we shall be like Him,' that is, Jesus. That's why we have a Quest for Excellence at Valley Christian Schools and why we don't claim to be excellent already. The Quest for Excellence™ means to become more like Jesus as we grow. He is the measure of excellence—the very nature, character and works of God."

The advertising consultants were stunned, and returned to the drawing boards.

THE KEY TO TRANSFORMATION

Later as I told this story to some parents, I added, "Christians all across the nation are praying for a spiritual transformation. I believe that God is answering that prayer through those who understand that Excellence Brings Influence™," I said, quoting the Quest for Excellence motto. "God has established Valley Christian Schools to launch students on their personal quests for excellence among the various professions and positions of influence where God is leading them to serve. They will become the most excellent professionals in their fields as they continue their quests to align themselves with God's standards rather than mere human standards. God's standards are much higher than any standard imaginable by human beings."

Learners:
   Are uniquely gifted with God-given talent
to achieve their God-intended purposes
                                    Chapter 20: 2

Christians who dedicate their professional ambitions to the cause of Christ have an advantage because they measure themselves against the ultimate standard of excellence—God's. With the bar set so high, many will naturally become the most influential professionals in their fields, because excellence always brings influence. This strategy will bring respect for the teachings of Jesus back to the marketplace of ideas and will realign the plausibility grids of those who would otherwise never seriously consider the claims and teachings of Christ. The teachings of Jesus will become plausible for the first time to millions who gain a growing respect for Christian professionals who are among the most accomplished people in their professions.

The strategy is clear, and it hasn't changed in 2,000 years.

"I beseech you therefore, brethren, by the mercies of God, that you present your bodies a living sacrifice, holy, acceptable to God, which is your reasonable service. And do not be conformed to this world, but be transformed by the renewing of your mind, that you may prove what is that good and acceptable and perfect will of God" (Romans 12:1–2).

And whatever you do, do it heartily, as to the Lord and not to men . . ." (Colossians 3:23).

The invasion is underway. Christians are beginning to take their places in all fields and professions with a fresh understanding that Excellence Brings Influence™. Rather than retreating from the world, believers are moving out as "salt" and "light" to transform their culture (see Matthew 5:13–16). Hollywood, Wall Street, the news media, the legal and medical professions, government, education, and business enterprises all represent areas where Christians of excellence and influence are on assignment to restore respect for the teachings of Jesus in the marketplace of ideas.

A PERSONAL MESSAGE TO THE READER

From God's perspective all that He has accomplished is very normal. From my perspective, I have witnessed the supernatural works of God through our lives. To God, all of His miraculous works at Valley Christian Schools are just normal every day occurrences. From my point of view, I remain in constant awe because I could have never imagined that I could lead in the development of a $100,000,000 school system in just over 10 years. Certainly God has given me the privilege of living the supernatural life - naturally. I am just an ordinary person that has the privilege of allowing our supernatural God to accomplish extraordinary achievements through the lives of those that I am privileged to serve with at Valley Christian Schools. Neither my parents nor their parents had the privilege of going to college or graduating from high school with their classmates. My father dropped out of high school during his junior year and eventually graduated by taking evening classes, nine years later. By the time I graduated from high school, no one expected anyone in our family to go to college. We did not know the difference between a vocational educational high school course and a college preparatory course. I did not have even one college preparatory course in high school.

But I had two great advantages. My mother's prayers and the promise of God's Word that "God hath chosen the foolish things of the world to confound the wise; and God hath chosen the weak things of the world to confound the things which are mighty (1 Corinthians 1:27 KJV).

I did not want to go to college. My parents loved me and were wonderful parents. They did not go to college, why would I? But as I prayed, God strongly directed me to apply to Bethany College in Santa Cruz, CA. I actually misspelled the word "college," "colledge" in the essay I submitted for admission. By some miracle I was admitted and the long journey that eventually took me to Pennsylvania State University and the University of San Francisco to receive a doctoral degree in special education and private school administration began.

I should not be surprised at what God accomplished through my life because Jesus said, "But seek first his kingdom and his righteousness, and all these things will be given to you as well" (Matthew 6:33). My life is proof that God has "chosen the foolish things of the world to confound the wise" and that **God works through ordinary people to do His supernatural work - naturally.**

Recently, VCS' Director of Technology, Mike Annab received an email from the Director of Technology of another fine school. He was discouraged and considering resignation because his Christian school leadership seemed to place more emphasis on academic quality than on Christian education.

Mike's response was profound.

Almost all of our most prized learning institutions began life with a Christian purpose and through the years, for one reason or a thousand reasons, turned secular. With regard to providing a top-notch education, there seems to be little compromise—but the building of character is replaced with teaching an ethics course. Our Christian/Catholic schools have probably the last great opportunity to infuse Christian values into our young people, the minority at that, but nonetheless those who attend our schools. Hopefully our students will become the decision makers, the future leaders, and the policy-makers. If our schools secularize to be more 'academic,' they'll follow the path of Harvard and may even become a top private high school with regard to SAT scores, etc. But lacking that eternal purpose, we'll be creating leaders who perhaps may lack God as a foundation of their spiritual lives. The question is why not have BOTH the high SAT scores, national recognition, AND retain all facets of a school's Christian character? It seems like there are some Christian schools that overlook that possibility altogether. In other words, they manufacture walls and procedures around themselves saying things like, 'I can't be successful without more computers. I can't have more computers without government grants. I can't get government grants without compromising my values. Therefore I must compromise my values in order to be successful.'

Dr. Daugherty's book debunks that myth in a big way. Anyway, it sounds like you've been in your position for a long time and that you really have a passion for Christian education. Stay the course. You can't help change the trends if you're not there, right? You may be the catalyst that turns this boat in the right direction. Just because you're not the President, CFO, or other executive administrator, remember one thing; when a ship sails, the slightest variation (perhaps no more than one small degree) over time, results in hundreds of miles. You CAN determine whether that is hundreds of miles off-course or hundreds of miles on-course.

May I encourage you? It does not matter how ordinary or dysfunctional your life may seem at this time. If you will call upon the Lord to develop and dedicate the talent and gifts that He has invested in your life to His service, you, too, will be in awe of how **God will live His supernatural life through you - naturally.**

A verse that speaks powerfully to me is:

"Call to Me, and I will answer you, and show you great and mighty things, which you do not know" (Jeremiah 33:3).

There is no doubt of God's faithful response to your sincere call. He will "show you great and mighty things, which you do not know." And then you, too, will be telling others how God is working through your ordinary life to accomplish extraordinary achievements.

"You are the light of the world. A city that is set on a hill cannot be hidden. Nor do they light a lamp and put it under a basket, but on a lamp stand, and it gives light to all who are in the house. Let your light so shine before men, that they may see your good works and glorify your Father in heaven" (Matthew 5:14–16).

CHAPTER 17

MOVING FROM INSPIRATION
TO IMPLEMENTATION
(BY ED SILVOSO)

Spiritual problems require spiritual solutions. No amount of secular training is sufficient to solve problems that have spiritual roots. There is only one way to do God's work effectively, and it is by and through the Spirit of God. To do it any other way is bound to have tragic consequences.

This became evident in the Old Testament when God commissioned two edifices for His presence to dwell. The first assignment went to Moses, who was asked to construct the Tent of the Covenant. The second went to Solomon, who was told to build the Temple. Both men successfully completed their assignments but with opposite results: Moses became a stronger person, whereas Solomon lost his faith and backslid spiritually.

How can it be that men to whom God entrusted such sacred projects met with fates so distinct? What caused Moses to grow stronger and Solomon weaker as they implemented on earth designs drafted by God in heaven?

The answer is found in whom these men relied on to do the task entrusted to them. Moses depended on Bezalel, an artisan who is the first person in the Bible filled with the Spirit of God (see Exodus 31). Bezalel was already a capable craftsman, but after being filled with the Spirit he was able to do his job in the fullness and power of God rather than just in his natural strengths and abilities. The Holy Spirit elevated what Bezalel had learned in trade school (most likely from his father as was the custom in biblical times) to a supernatural height.

On the other hand, Solomon hired pagan temple builders, mainly from his heathen friend Hiram, the king of Lebanon, to build God's house. This was a most unfortunate contradiction since God is holy and Solomon hired ungodly people to erect His earthly dwelling. I am sure what motivated Solomon was the fact that these professionals were the best contemporary craftsmen, but they were not filled with the Spirit of God and as such they depended exclusively on their own abilities rather than God's. Worse yet, being unbelievers, they became channels for evil into Solomon's project and eventually into his life as well.

In the preceding chapters we have seen how God made known His will for VCS and how Cliff Daugherty and his team followed His leading until that initial vision took shape and became tangible. In essence, the preceding chapters chronicle how natural people learned to live supernaturally. Like Bezalel, Cliff and his associates already had a level of natural knowledge and expertise, but they did not limit themselves to it. Instead, time and again, when facing obstacles that superseded their natural abilities, they reached up to God to access the spirit of revelation in the knowledge of Jesus Christ so that His will would be done on earth as it is already done in heaven.

In the following section you will be introduced to the principles, practices and core educational values that came into focus at VCS as a result of its leadership following God's guidance day after day. This is how they won many battles that at first looked lost until new spiritual insights illuminated unseen paths that led them out of the wilderness.

The principles, practices and values described here are like footprints in the sand. Those footprints are not the person who walked on the sand but they reflect the path that he followed, and as such, provide a blueprint for you to initiate a similar supernatural journey - naturally.

In my book *Prayer Evangelism* I state that a successful visionary is one who rather than becoming discouraged by setbacks uses them as a place on which to plant and raise the banner of faith. The visionary is never limited by the way things look in the natural because he is intentionally focused on what he sees with the eyes of the Spirit as he accesses the supernatural.

This is why a successful visionary is one who seems to have a manageable case of spiritual schizophrenia. When he or she looks at things in the natural he knows that there is no way, humanly speaking, that it can be done. But as he considers the same situation through the eyes of the Spirit he believes, beyond any doubt, that it can and more importantly that it will be done. The reason? Because God says so and faith is the assurance of things hoped for, the manifestation of things still invisible. That is how the visionary constantly zigzags between the impossible and the possible, like a sailor tacking through contrary winds to move the boat forward by using them to his advantage.

In *Anointed for Business* I describe four levels in which Christians find themselves in the marketplace today.

At the very lowest level are those who are struggling (and failing) in the workplace. Every day they suffer brutal onslaughts that cause them to lose rather than to gain ground. Even though some well-meaning spiritual counselors may try to justify this state of failure by pointing out that it builds Christian character, this does not constitute abundant life. Like General Patton told a group of new recruits during WWII, "The secret to winning the war is not dying for your country but making the enemy die for his country."

The next level up consists of Christians who apply biblical principles in the marketplace. This is where the vast majority of believers are today. I would say as many as 90% of them are at this level, but the problem is that they apply biblical principles not so much to change the marketplace but to keep the marketplace from changing them. In other words, they have settled for a draw, but no team can win the championship by ending every game in a draw. We need to apply biblical principles to win!

This takes us to the next level: Christians who apply biblical principles in the marketplace to do business in the power and in the fullness of the Holy Spirit. This means that when they go to work, they expect to be led by the Holy Spirit. They count on God empowering them and providing them with supernatural insights. These folks will never surrender but press forward, in prayer, intercession, supplication, and spiritual perseverance, until the gates of Hades blocking their path become a pile of debris. When confronted with the gates of hell, they call on the Holy Spirit's supernatural weapons that are mighty in God for the destruction of such fortresses.

And finally, the highest level consists of Christians who operate in the power and the fullness of the Holy Spirit to bring transformation to the marketplace, and in the case of this book, to the field of education. Their objective is not simply to have a good Christian school but, like in the case of Cliff Daugherty and the leadership at VCS, to transform the way education is done in the nation. These folks have come to understand at the deepest level that Jesus came to seek and save not just the lost, but that which was lost. And that means everything that was lost in the Garden of Eden when sin first entered.

They know that Jesus did not die just for people but for the world; that John 3:16 states that God loves not just the world population but also the world itself and its institutions. In essence, they have come to understand that the marketplace is redeemed by the expiatory death of Jesus and now must be reclaimed by the Church. This is why they can exercise God-given authority through the power of the Holy Spirit to crumble the defiant gates of Hades into nothing more than a pile of rubble.

The following section outlines powerful principles, practices and values that are essential for this to happen and how, after embracing them, you can also live the supernatural life - naturally in your own sphere of influence.

NOTE TO THE READER

The reader is encouraged to read Chapter 18 or Chapter 19 but not both chapters since the content will appear redundant. The principles and practices described in Chapter 18 are specifically written for the development of comprehensive Christian high schools. For other endeavors or professional pursuits, the reader may want to skip Chapter 18 and proceed directly to Chapter 19.

CHAPTER 18
FIVE PRINCIPLES AND PRACTICES OF VALLEY CHRISTIAN SCHOOLS' QUEST FOR EXCELLENCE™

As the Lord built Valley Christian Schools—from a $2.5 million budget with deficits up to $320,000 and inferior rented facilities in 1991 to a $25 million budget with new facilities and assets exceeding $100 million in 2006—five principles and their associated practices emerged. These principles and practices seem to reside at the heart of Valley Christian Schools' Quest for Excellence™.

These principles are offered as a model for Christian school leaders to develop extraordinary high schools that prepare youth to pursue extraordinary achievements among the professions of influence in order that they may restore respect to the cause of Christ in the marketplace of ideas.

1. **Maintain an Integrated Christ-Centered Focus on Excellence in All Academic and Co-curricular Programs**

    A. Inform students that God is preparing them to restore respect for Christian faith in the marketplace of ideas, with the goal of fulfilling Christ's commission to "Go to the people of all nations and make them my disciples" through their personal Quests for Excellence (Matthew 28:19a, CEV).

    B. Equip and challenge students to integrate socially and professionally into the culture—not to retreat from the world. Rather than trying to shelter students from the evils of the world, quality Christian schools progressively expose students to the world as "salt" and "light" (Matthew 5:13–16; John 17:15–23).

C. Excellence Brings Influence™. Our students' personal commitment to excellence—girded with the motivation that "Whatever you do, do it heartily, as to the Lord and not to men" (Colossians 3:23)—will ensure their pursuit of extraordinary achievements in their emerging personal and professional spheres of influence.

D. Some strategies in pursuit of this effort include:

1. Train students to be individually internalized Christians that reflect the reason and the passion of their faith.

2. Develop a school culture of "grace and truth" (John 1:14).

3. Sustain and acknowledge the importance of an intercessory prayer ministry involving parents and students, and nurture respect for God-appointed prayer intercessors.

4. Require students to take four years of Bible courses that address the varied spiritual needs of students.

5. Allow students to internalize Christian faith through personal choice, rather than using an indoctrination approach to inculcate religious instruction.

6. Ensure that the school remains a safe place to sincerely express and explore doubts about God and to internalize a personal faith.

7. Admit students who meet behavioral and academic standards and are committed to "give the Lord Jesus a fair hearing," with the support

of their parents. Parents need not be Christian but must agree to support the school's Christian philosophy of education and allow their children personally to accept the Christian faith. The truth is so compelling that most students become committed Christians regardless of their parents' beliefs; some parents also accept Christ.

8. Maintain admissions policies that seek to match the God-given talent of students to the school's extraordinary programs, faculty, and coaches.

9. Achieve and maintain accreditation from the Association of Christian Schools International (ACSI) and a regional organization such as the Western Association of Schools and Colleges.

10. Sustain an interdenominational focus that serves the entire Christian church community. Focus on the elements of historically held Christian faith that all Bible-believing Christians have held in common throughout the history of the Church. Do not allow advocacy for or debate about beliefs involving denominational distinctions/differences.

2. **Develop a *Comprehensive* Christian High School Committed to the Quest for Excellence™ in Every Area: The Whole is More Than the Sum of the Parts**

A. Develop outstanding programs to attract students—don't wait until enough students are enrolled to justify the program.

B. Provide all program offerings normally associated with outstanding secular high schools, but insist that each program offer qualities that parents can find only through your Christian school.

C. Develop comprehensive program offerings ranging from those for students with special educational and vocational needs to a complete college-preparatory program including honors and advanced placement college-level courses. The school must develop the most challenging programs, such as a symphonic orchestra, concert band, jazz band and a marching field show competition band; a complete theater program; and all of the critical athletic programs including aquatics, baseball, basketball, cross country, football, golf, soccer, softball, tennis, track, volleyball, wrestling, and more.

3. **Plan Such Exceptional Programs and Specialized Facilities that God Will Attract Extraordinarily Capable People to Help Fund Their Development**

The rationale for this principle includes these insights:

A. Extraordinary people of extraordinary means are looking for extraordinary projects where they can invest their resources in an extraordinary cause with extraordinary results. These godly stewards are not attracted to projects that are "just as good" as those at the local public high school. They want to invest in an excellent school, not an ordinary school. It is harder to fund an ordinary school than an extraordinary "heavenly" school. Only people of ordinary means will contribute to an ordinary school, and even an ordinary school is most often beyond their means.

B. God's plans are always humanly impossible and amazingly extraordinary. Christian school administrators should determine to discover God's plans, document them, share them, and then watch how God develops His own vision. God is always willing and completely able to fund His plans and ideas. In contrast, even though our own plans are so much smaller than God's, our ideas are limited to human resources.

C. Christian schools sometimes fall short in receiving all of God's generous funding because His ideas seem so massive that we are afraid to put God-given dreams on the drawing board, succumbing to the notion that "we could never afford it." When there seems to be a shortage of money (as occurred during the VCS Quest for Excellence™ planning phase), exercise faith and refuse to downsize the plans to fit the limitations of the school's immediate resources. Keep the plans that God seems to confirm, and "wait upon the Lord" for His resources (see Isaiah 40:31). Before curtailing plans for lack of funding, consider extending the time horizon for God's provision by building in phases if necessary.

D. Have courage to begin moving forward with the resources at hand in anticipation of what God will provide to implement the plan. (In most cases, it was all I could do to get enough money to pay our architects, engineers, environmental consultants, legal counsel, and other planners just to complete the plans for a project.) If you can get a glimpse of what God wants to do, plan the project and He will provide the resources and the right people to accomplish His vision. Do not allow the thought that "if I can barely afford to plan a project, how can I ever afford to build it?" to kill a project that God wants you to complete. While planning the project, move forward as if there is no shortage of funds. In fact, God has all of the resources for His projects even though you cannot see them until they are needed (see Philippians 4:19). This idea, simply stated, is, "Plan it and God will build it."

F. Kevin Compton of Kleiner Perkins, a leading venture capital firm, told me, "There is no shortage of money; there is only a shortage of great ideas." God has extraordinary plans for all Christians who "seek first the kingdom of God," and He does not have a shortage of resources to achieve His purposes. He wants to achieve His purposes through Christians who will "do all in the name of the Lord Jesus, giving thanks to God" and "do it heartily, as to the Lord and not to men" (Colossians 3:17, 23). Christian schools often have a shortage of money because they have a shortage of God-given dreams and documented plans. Get God's dream, commit the plans to paper, and expect God to fund the project by speaking to extraordinarily capable people to help make it happen. God has extraordinary plans and extraordinary resources. When leaders are in line with His heavenly purposes, they will discover God's great plans and His great provision.

G. A minimum of twenty-five (smaller school) and up to fifty or more acres are needed for a comprehensive secondary campus. Some of the facilities that should be included in the dream are:

   1. Art classrooms: one or more rooms for each 500 to 600 students

   2. Athletic programs, including:
◊   Baseball: ideally two fields, although one may be off campus nearby
◊   Basketball: gym(s) required
◊   Cross Country

◊   Field and Track: track required, ideally all-weather
◊   Football: field required
◊   Golf: usually in cooperation with a local course
◊   Soccer: field required
◊   Softball: field required
◊   Swimming and Water Polo: school or community pool required
◊   Tennis: six courts needed
◊   Volleyball: gym(s) required
◊   Wrestling: mat facilities required

3. Band and Choral rooms, with recording and storage facilities: one room for each 500 to 600 students
4. College and career counseling facilities: at least one counselor for each 250 to 300 students
5. Communications department: radio, television, film, journalism, yearbook, and photography
6. Dance studio(s), adjacent to the theater with high quality dance floors and changing facilities: one dance studio for each 600 to 800 students
7. Gymnasium(s), including a large mat room for cheer as well as wrestling: ideally a large multi-court gym for at least 1,000 fans and chapel services, and a smaller multi-court practice gym–outdoor basketball and volleyball courts should supplement indoor gyms with one added court for every 250 to 350 students
8. Language laboratories—integrated into the media center and the foreign language classrooms

9. Library: outstanding balanced collection with no fewer than 10,000 books (smaller school) or ten to twenty books per student minimum
10. Science laboratories: specialized anatomy, biology, chemistry, and physics labs; one lab for every 200 to 300 students
11. Technology: integrated "state of the art" equipment and resources within the reach of every student as needed
12. Theater: a minimum of 200 seats
13. Training facilities for a certified trainer or training staff: one trainer or assistant trainer for every 400 to 500 students
14. Weight and strengthening facilities: One thousand square feet or more for every 400 to 500 students

4. **Maintain an Exceptionally Qualified and Properly Compensated Executive Leadership Team, Faculty, and Staff**

A. Teachers should possess appropriate degrees with a major or minor in their areas of instruction.
B. Teachers should teach no more than one or two subjects, with rare exceptions. Poor instructional quality most often results from one teacher teaching more than two subjects.
C. Provide a staff development program.
D. Cultivate a qualified executive leadership team, including a Chief Executive Officer, Chief Financial Officer, and Development Officer. Depending of the size of the school, positions such as a Director of Curriculum, Director of Technology, a Human Resources Director, Operations Director and other positions may report to the executive team as needed. The CEO/superintendent

should be an experienced educational visionary with a master's or doctoral degree. A qualified CFO should have CPA or MBA credentials, with proven executive leadership experience. The most effective development officers are masters at cultivating major donors. It is of great advantage to the school if the Director of Development is deeply rooted in the community. Valley Christian schools named the Director of Development–Chancellor.

5. **Measure, Monitor, and Manage All Elements of Quality to Put the School on a Solid Management and Business Foundation "Not slothful in business; fervent in spirit; serving the Lord" (Romans 12:11, KJV)**

   A. Develop measures to chart progress in the Quest for Excellence™ for all critical areas of academic, program, student, and staff performance along with measures of perceived satisfaction by students, staff, and parents.

   B. Showcase innovative programs and student achievements through the highest quality publications and events.

   C. Develop comprehensive programs to attract at least 400 high school students to achieve a minimally comprehensive program and to balance the budget (VCS' experience).

   D. Charge enough tuition to meet all operational expenses, fund innovative programs that will attract outstanding students and families, and avoid crisis fundraising.

   E. The test for every department is when people say, "If you want that (a distinctive program or quality), you must go to (Your School Name) Christian School."

F. Promote fundraising that immediately adds quality to the school in the form of creative programs, improved staff compensation, or exceptional facilities. Avoid crises fundraising to fund operations! It inadvertently broadcasts financial incompetence.

G. Create an economic "dashboard" that provides a business "snapshot" to monitor leading indicators of economic health on a monthly, quarterly, and annual basis, for the entire school system and for each school. Some indicators include:
    1. Total assets, net assets, unrestricted cash assets
    2. Restricted cash assets and liquidity ratio (cash-to-debt ratio)
    3. Current enrollment compared to budgeted enrollment
    4. Student-to-teacher ratios
    5. Debt service coverage ratio (net income adjusted by non-cash items/debt service cash expense)
    6. Net income per student
    7. Staff cost per student
    8. Instructional cost per student
    9. Tuition and fees per student
    10. Donations per student, other revenue per student

H. Maintain a five-year fiscal forecast on a spreadsheet that projects tuition, salaries, cash reserves, program and operational expenditures, and capital costs. Project the margin effects of every financial decision on the five-year model.

CHAPTER 19

FIVE PRINCIPLES AND PRACTICES FOR CHRISTIAN PROFESSIONALS

Chapter 18 details the five principles and their associated practices that I observed from the Valley Christian Schools' experience as we have journeyed on our own Quest for Excellence™. The elements of these principles and practices can be generalized to apply to many professional endeavors, not just the development of a top-quality Christian school.

These Quest for Excellence principles and practices are a model for Christian professionals to pursue extraordinary achievements in many fields. Christian professionals can restore respect for the cause of Christ in the marketplace of ideas and transform 21ˢᵗ century culture, because Excellence Brings Influence™.

1. **Maintain a Christ-Centered Focus on Excellence in Every Aspect of Your Personal and Professional Endeavors**

    A. Remember that God wants you to help restore respect for Christian faith in the marketplace of ideas. Expect to integrate socially and professionally into the culture—not to retreat from the world. Believers are to be "salt" and "light" (Matthew 5:13–16; John 17:15–23). Focus on the goal of fulfilling Christ's commission to "Go to the people of all nations and make them my disciples" (Matthew 28:19a, CEV).

210 DR. CLIFFORD E. DAUGHERTY

      B. Develop a culture of "grace and truth" throughout your professional sphere of influence (John 1:14).

      C. Support intercessory prayer involving employees, co-workers, staff, customers, and friends.

      D. Maintain a professionally safe environment that encourages people to practice, discuss, express, and explore their spiritual beliefs.

      E. Achieve and maintain accreditation, licensing, certification, endorsements, or other appropriate professional credentials that give assurance of your commitment to professional quality.

      F. Maintain a gracious focus of prayer for the felt needs of all people, regardless of their religious perspective. Do not allow disputes about religious beliefs in the workplace.

2. Offer Leading Quality Professional Products and Services with a Comprehensive View of Your Market Niche

      A. Recognize that the whole is more than the sum of the parts—alliances with other providers may achieve a competitive advantage.

      B. Develop outstanding programs to attract clients—don't wait until you get enough demand to justify the product or service.

      C. Offer distinctive qualities that clients can find only through your products or services.

3. Plan Such Exceptional Products, Services, and Specialized Facilities That God Will Attract Extraordinarily Capable People to Your Team

The rationale for this principle includes these insights:

      A. Extraordinary people of extraordinary means are looking for extraordinary projects where they can invest their resources in an extraordinary cause with extraordinary results. These godly stewards are not attracted to projects that are "just as good" as those at any similar organization. They want to invest in an excellent—not an ordinary—opportunity. It is harder to fund an ordinary endeavor than an extraordinary "heavenly" one. Only people of ordinary means will join an ordinary venture, and even an ordinary endeavor is often beyond their means.

B. God's plans are always humanly impossible and amazingly extraordinary. Christian professionals should determine to discover God's plans, document them, share them, and then watch how God develops His own vision. God is always willing and completely able to fund His plans and ideas. In contrast, even though our own plans are so much smaller than God's, our ideas are limited to human resources.

C. Professional endeavors sometimes fall short in receiving all of God's generous funding because His ideas seem so massive that we are afraid to put God-given dreams on the drawing board, succumbing to the notion that "we could never afford it."

D. When there seems to be a shortage of money, exercise faith and refuse to downsize your plans to fit your immediate resources. Keep the plans that God seems to confirm, and "wait upon the Lord" for His resources (see Isaiah 40:31).

E. Before curtailing plans for lack of funding, consider extending the time horizon for God's provision by moving ahead in phases if necessary.

F. Have courage to begin moving forward with the resources at hand in anticipation of what God will provide to implement the plan. (In most cases, it was all I could do to get enough money to pay our architects, engineers, environmental consultants, legal counsel, and other planners just to complete the plans for a project.) If you can get a glimpse of what God wants to do, plan the project and He will provide the resources and the right people to accomplish His vision. This idea, simply stated, is, "Plan it and God will build it."

G. Resist the thought, "If we can barely afford to plan the project, how can we ever afford to build it?"

H. While planning the project, move forward as if there is no shortage of funds. In fact, God has all of the resources for His projects even though you cannot see them until they are needed (see Philippians 4:19).

I. Kevin Compton of Kleiner Perkins, a leading venture capital firm, told me, "There is no shortage of money; there is only a shortage of great ideas." God has extraordinary plans for all Christians who "seek first the kingdom of God," and He does not have a shortage of resources to achieve His purposes. He wants to achieve His purposes through Christians who will "do all in the name of the Lord Jesus, giving thanks to God" and "do it heartily, as to the Lord and not to men" (Colossians 3:17, 23).

J. Christians often have a shortage of money because they have a shortage of God-given dreams and documented plans. Get God's dream, commit the plans to paper, and expect God to fund the project by speaking to extraordinarily capable people to help make it happen. God has extraordinary plans and extraordinary resources. When leaders are in line with His heavenly purposes, they will discover God's great plans and His great provision.

4. Attract and Maintain an Exceptionally Qualified and Well Compensated Team

A. Team members should have appropriate educational credentials or other documented skills indicating their exceptional competence.

B. Team members should concentrate on their specific areas of expertise and gifting.

C. Provide a staff development program.

D. Cultivate a qualified executive leadership team with proven experience. At a minimum every business needs an insightful, visionary CEO and a qualified CFO with CPA or MBA credentials. Small businesses may contract services with an outstanding accounting firm.

5. Measure, Monitor, and Manage All Elements of Quality to Put the Organization on a Solid Management and Business Foundation
"Not slothful in business; fervent in spirit; serving the Lord" (Romans 12:11, KJV)

A. Develop measures to chart progress on the quality of all critical areas of products and services along with measures of perceived satisfaction by staff and customers or clients.

B. Showcase innovative programs and achievements through the highest quality publications and events.

C. Charge enough money for products and services to meet all operational expenses and fund innovative programs that will attract outstanding customers and clients.

D. Offer such distinctive products and services that customers and clients will say, "If you want that, you must go to or have [insert your name, the name of your business, or your products or services]."

E. Create an economic "dashboard" that provides a business "snapshot" to monitor leading indicators of economic health on a monthly, quarterly, and annual basis. Some indicators include:

1. Total assets, net assets, unrestricted cash assets
2. Restricted cash assets, liquidity ratio (cash-to-debt ratio)
3. Current income compared to budgeted income
4. Debt service coverage ratio (net income adjusted by non-cash items/debt service cash expense)

F. Maintain a five-year fiscal forecast on a spreadsheet that projects income, salaries, cash reserves, program and operational expenditures, and capital costs. Project the margin effects of every financial decision on the five-year model.

G. Make investments in your business or profession that give a competitive edge through added quality in the form of creative products, services, or exceptional facilities.

CHAPTER 20
CORE EDUCATIONAL VALUES

Valley Christian Schools' core educational values are summarized in five statements.

THE QUEST FOR EXCELLENCE™
At Valley Christian Schools, we understand excellence to be the nature, character, and works of God. Quality education involves teaching students at their individual levels of understanding and offering instruction at a pace that ensures success. The purpose of Christian education is for students to internalize Christian values and to develop their God-given talents to achieve God's unique purposes for their lives.

PREAMBLE
- Whereas Valley Christian Schools is founded on Christian values as found in the Bible and reflected in the life and teachings of Jesus Christ, and
- Whereas Valley Christian Schools was founded by God to fulfill the mission and purpose as reflected in the school's documented statements, and
- Whereas Valley Christian Schools subscribe to the Association of Christian Schools International's Statement of Faith,
- Now therefore the following practices and truths are held as core educational values of Valley Christian Schools.

FIVE CORE EDUCATIONAL VALUES

PARENTS:

1. Are the primary educators of their children under God
   A. Support the Christian philosophy and policies of VCS
   B. Delegate authority to VCS for the education of their children

LEARNERS:

2. Are uniquely gifted with God-given talent to achieve their God-intended purposes
   A. Are willing to give the Christian faith a "fair hearing" or
   B. Are growing in their faith

SCHOOL LEADERS AND TEACHERS:

3. Serve as loving Christian role models that guide learners through positive relationships
   A. Are called and gifted by God's Spirit to teach
   B. Match God-given student talents with a wide range of extraordinary learning opportunities
   C. Are professionally prepared
   D. Remain life-long learners
   E. View parents as the primary educators of their children under God
   F. Pray regularly for and with their students
4. Help students discover their unique God-given talents through comprehensive innovative programs
   A. Provide for a wide range of ability levels
   B. Recognize the multiple intelligences of students
   C. Incorporate varied ongoing assessments of learning with the goal of meeting the unique

needs of each student

D. Include an interdisciplinary/cross-curricular instructional design

5. Develop the God-given talents of students to achieve their God-intended life's work

   A. Define measurable, grade-level academic standards for each subject

   B. Measure each student's academic achievement for each subject and grade level

   C. Facilitate the expression of Truth and Life through the discovery of Christian values as found in the Bible and reflected in the life and teachings of Jesus Christ among all disciplines and co-curricular activities

   D. Involve the cognitive, affective, and kinesthetic domains in learning

   E. Apply multi-modal/multi-sensory instructional methods such as project-based learning and other similar strategies

   F. Encourage ethnic, cultural, and socioeconomic harmony within a diverse school population

CHAPTER 21
ACHIEVEMENTS OF EXCELLENCE

Valley Christian Schools, its faculty and students have received numerous awards and recognition for achievements in a wide range of areas since launching the Quest for Excellence™ during the 1990–91 school year. Based in the insight that Excellence Brings Influence™, it became the schools' goal to reflect the nature, character, and works of God to our community and the world. Here is a sample of various student and school achievements during recent years:

- In 2002 the high school was selected by Cal Hi Sports as the California State Athletic School of the Year. (Division IV)
- Valley Christian High School athletes have won seventy-six league championships and ten Central Coast Sectional (CCS) championships.
- VCHS boasts the highest-ranked high school football team in the San Francisco Bay and San Jose areas. After winning the fourth consecutive CCS championship, www.Calpreps.com ranked the Valley Warriors as the number one ranked high school football team in California on the morning of December 3, 2005. All nine hundred ninety-five high school football teams in California were ranked.
- VCS teams won back-to-back CCS basketball championships for 2003 and 2004.
- The girls' soccer team won the CCS championship title in 2004 and 2006.
- The girls' softball team was ranked fourth in California in 2006 among all high schools.
- Splash, Valley Christian Schools' U.S. Olympic prep-

aration swim team, placed first in competition at the Santa Clara International Swim Center in 2004.

- Valley Christian High School's field show competition band claimed the state championship for AA/AAA class at the Western Band Association field show competition in both 2003 and 2004, along with many sweepstakes trophies in the band competitions.
- Valley Christian High School's symphonic band took first place in the Disney World band competition sweepstakes in the spring of 2005.
- Seven students were selected for the All-State Honor Band in the 2004–2005 school year.
- Valley Christian Schools' dance, theater, orchestra, and vocal departments generate some of the most amazing high school theater productions imaginable. The theater won the prestigious award for best staging from the Center for Performing Arts in 2005.
- Radio students manage and produce programming for KVCH, the world's first high school radio station to broadcast live on the Internet twenty-four hours a day, beginning in 1995.
- The VCHS yearbook has been an ACSI first-place winner in many categories for years.
- The high school newspaper, *The Warrior,* has received a first-place ranking for the past three years in the American High School Newspaper Awards.
- Sixty-eight percent of Valley Christian High School's 2004 graduating class of more than 280 students qualified for admission to the University of California. An added twenty-eight percent qualified for California State University. More than ninety-five percent of graduates enroll in college, and many are accepted into some of the top universities in the nation.

- The 2006 graduating class boasted several National Achievement and National Merit Scholar finalists, and well over $10 million in college scholarship offers.
- In the 2005–2006 scholastic year, fifteen advanced placement college-level courses were offered, in many cases with more than one class period per course. During the 2005 a total of 337 students, many who took multiple AP courses, enjoyed pass rates for college credit that more than doubled California high school averages. Students took more than 600 AP examinations during 2006.
- The Junior High Jazz band won the 2006 Western States Reno Jazz Championship.
- In 2004 the United States Department of Education bestowed the "No Child Left Behind" Blue Ribbon Award on Valley Christian High School, the only private high school in California and one of only four in the nation to receive the prestigious Blue Ribbon Award that year. Among many other requirements, VCHS was able to show evidence that student scholastic achievement scores were among the top ten percent in the nation.
- In 2006 Jake Viramontez won 1st place in the National Student Television Network Sprint Competition representing the film, TV, and video productions department at VCS.
- Several students are nationally and world ranked in the youth division for track and field.

CHAPTER 22

HOW TO HAVE FAITH FOR THE IMPOSSIBLE AND EXPERIENCE GOD'S SUPERNATURAL WORK— NATURALLY

Throughout our faith journey, we at Valley Christian Schools have learned many faith lessons about living a supernatural life - naturally. God has accomplished His wonderful works through us even when it seemed impossible. These principles have timeless truth for anyone desiring to have faith to pursue God unwaveringly, pray persistently, and witness His amazing involvement in everyday life.

We believe the power of God is available to anyone who will seek Him on His terms. We can never put a leash on God to lead Him where we want to go. On the contrary, the key to experiencing His power is to surrender ourselves to the Lord for His purposes, dying to ourselves and inviting the excellence of Christ to live through us—supernaturally.

Here are some of the lessons I've learned through God's amazing miraculous works at Valley Christian Schools:

1. Get to Know The "Boss"

Devote yourself to knowing God at increasingly deeper levels. The more you get to know His nature, character and works, the more He will accomplish His supernatural work through you—naturally.

2. **Stay In The Book**

Feed your soul on God's written Word. Maintain high regard for God's ability to guide and direct through the eternal principles of Scripture. Memorize passages so God can use them to speak to you at any time. I have committed to reading God's Word for at least five minutes every day. Five minutes often leads to much more time. When I read, I am praying for God to direct me personally through His Holy Spirit.

3. **Stay Tuned And Keep Talking**

Pray regularly as a spiritual discipline. Give God your full attention so He has an opportunity to speak to you about anything, including matters that are not already on your mind. As you develop a God-consciousness in all you do, you will find it easier to keep your ear tuned to God's Spirit and maintain a dialog with Him throughout the day. Listen for God to speak into your thoughts in every situation. Even if the answer seems obvious, do not ignore the possibility that He may have something to say, if only to confirm your thoughts. He may surprise you.

4. **Get A Heart Transplant**

Allow God to transplant His thoughts, desires and purposes into your heart. Be willing to let go of previous assumptions and practices, even those long held. In particular, do not confuse personal or cultural preferences with timeless Christian principles.

"And I will give you a new heart with new and right desires, and I will put a new spirit in you. I will take out your stony heart of sin and give you a new, obedient heart. And I will put my Spirit in you so you will obey my laws and do whatever I command" (Ezekiel 36:26–27 NLT).

5. Walk In The Light

Ask God to shine the light of the Holy Spirit on any area of your heart that needs housecleaning. Ask Jesus to clean house by confessing your sins immediately. Submit to God's will, and stay in right relationship with Him moment by moment so that nothing blocks your communication. Keep in proper submission to people who have spiritual authority over you. Make sure all your personal relationships are in order since the kingdom of God is a kingdom of righteous, loving relationships with God, our neighbors and our selves.

6. Get A Clue!

Understand that a God-given vision is getting a glimpse of what God wants to do through you. When God gives you a vision, He will give you the faith and the means to see it happen.

7. Think Big

Expect that any vision from God is bigger than any dream you could ever imagine. Depend on God's resources rather than just what you have on hand or in view. If you can easily accomplish a vision yourself, it is probably not of God.

8. Mission Impossible?

Don't dismiss "impossible" options. Likewise, do not assume that the opening of promising new doors means that God wants you to walk through them; pray and ask God to confirm His direction.

9. Expect Confirmation

God sometimes confirms His message through a persistent, deeper sense of "knowing," or He may speak through Scripture reading, or through various circumstances of life. On occasion, He confirms His guidance through other people and often through a combination of means. When you sense that God is speaking, do not be afraid to ask Him for confirmation and correct understanding. When you sense you have received confirmation and correct understanding, move ahead in courage to obey what you have heard. Once you have confidence about God's will for a particular situation, it becomes easier to persist in prayer, faith, and action toward its accomplishment. An often-repeated pattern for me is:

    A. Confirmation through a passage of scripture that seems to come alive

    B. Support from my wife, Kris, or other loved ones

    C. The presence of a prayer burden for the project by our intercessory prayer group

    D. Agreement by our administrative team and our Valley Christian Schools Board

10. Let God Speak For Himself

Do not be surprised when you cannot convince others to support a God-sized project. After all, a rational person would immediately say that any of God's plans seem impossible. Trust that He knows how to communicate with people that are needed for the project in ways that are personally meaningful to them.

11. Pay The Price

As God leads, be willing to sacrifice and give all toward the fulfillment of God's purposes. When God wants to stretch your faith, the process is often uncomfortable, even painful, requiring you to see and do things differently and seemingly unnaturally. It is not unusual for you, a rational person, to question your sanity if you are like Noah trying to build an Ark on dry ground when it had never rained in the history of the world; like Moses trying to lead millions of people across the Red Sea without even one boat; or, like aged Abraham and barren Sara trying to have as many children as there are stars in the sky and grains of sand on the shore. Trust Him to take care of your needs and your reputation in pursuit of the vision. Take heed; the more vision God gives to you, the more you are responsible for accomplishing. As Jesus said, " . . . to whom much is given, from him much will be required" (Luke 12:48).

12. "Wait Upon The Lord"

Since only God can do His work, "wait on the Lord" to do it. You cannot force progress even if you try. Position yourself for God to act, then watch and wait expectantly for what God will do. Allow time for God to do His work in His way. Allow Him to teach you through trials and challenges. Wait, but do not give up on the vision. God often gives progressive disclosure to His vision. It seems that the larger the vision, the longer the lead-time between seeing the vision and doing the vision. The lead-time allows adequate prayer, personal spiritual growth and planning. We were led to purchase the land for Valley Christian Schools ten years before God opened the door for city approvals and for construction to begin. It seemed that the Skyway campus vision was dead and buried. But just about the time I was beginning to question whether I had misunderstood God's vision, God powerfully resurrected the project. I have discovered that God allows all to appear lost just before He shows up and does His miraculous work. I call them Cliff hangers! It is a great reminder that He is God and He uses these circumstances to grow our faith.

13. Forget Plan B

Insist on going forward according to God's "A Team" plans. When obstacles or setbacks arise, pray and ask God to show you how He wants to deal with the situation. Believe that He does not want to settle for Plan B. Do not succumb to fear. God's vision is never lacking His provision. Be open to creative and unprecedented solutions. Remember that "plans made in heaven are never ten feet too short!" (A Chapter 11 reference)

14. Call In The Air Force

The Bible refers to Satan as "the mighty prince of the power of the air" (Ephesians 2:2). The enemy always opposes God's work.

"For we are not fighting against people made of flesh and blood, but against the evil rulers and authorities of the unseen world, against those mighty powers of darkness who rule this world, and against wicked spirits in the heavenly realms" (Ephesians 6:12 NLT).

I have learned that He appoints prayer intercessors to call in air cover of His angelic hosts for His faithful warriors on the front lines. Watch for and honor the intercessors that God assigns to pray for you and the vision you share. It is very helpful to pray weekly with an intercessory team as God leads. Keep your prayer team informed of your vision, your prayer requests and on how God is answering prayer so they can pray strategically. Allow God to guide you corporately as well as individually.

"Pray at all times and on every occasion in the power of the Holy Spirit. Stay alert and be persistent in your prayers for all Christians everywhere. And pray for me, too" (Ephesians 6:18–19a NLT).

The enemy is no match for God's angelic Air Force and the Lord will defeat the "mighty prince of the power of the air" through prayer and the air cover of His angelic hosts. Every phase of God's work at Valley Christian Schools required a breakthrough in prayer to achieve success. When circumstances, human weaknesses and dark forces seem to block God's purposes, partner with God-appointed prayer intercessors to call in the Air Force, God's angelic hosts!

"Praise Him, all His angels; Praise Him, all His hosts!" (Psalm 148:2).

"Restore us, O Lord God of hosts; Cause Your face to shine, And we shall be saved!" (Psalm 80:19).

"The Lord of hosts is with us; The God of Jacob is our refuge" (Psalm 46:11).

God assigns His angels to each of us as children, and they are at His command to help us achieve His purposes throughout our lives as we pray and seek to serve Him.

"Take heed that you do not despise one of these little ones, for I say to you that in heaven their angels always see the face of My Father who is in heaven" (Matthew 18:10).

(If you would like to study the subject of angels in more depth, see Billy Graham's book *Angels, Angels, Angels.*)

15. Keep the Faith

Do not allow obstacles to stop you or to damage your faith. Your faith will soar if instead you see obstacles as opportunities for God to demonstrate His miraculous power. Let Him reassure you about His desire and intention to accomplish His highest purposes in whatever way He chooses. Remember that faith is a gift of the Holy Spirit, and until God gives us the gift for each of His works, we cannot manufacture the faith. The Spirit gives special faith. . . ." (1 Corinthians 12:9 NLT).

16. Duke It Out

Give yourself permission to wrestle with your doubts, and to work through the "why" questions. Ask God to help you understand scriptural truths that apply to

230 DR. CLIFFORD E. DAUGHERTY

your situation. Ask God for the faith to make a whole-hearted commitment to move forward in the face of unanswered questions like, "Where will we get the money?"

17. Tap G reat Talent

Do your homework to discover and engage the finest talent to help move the vision forward. The initial price tag is usually higher, but such quality usually improves the bottom line before long. It helps to ask the right questions. Three examples are:

A. When VCS needed a development officer, we asked, "Which Christian in our community is best connected and positioned to help raise millions of dollars to build a school?"

B. When we needed someone to put the logos on our gyms I asked, "Who put the logos on the Stanford University and University of California, Berkley gyms?"

C. When we needed sound systems I asked, "Who installed the sound systems for the San Jose Arena?"

Needless to say, God has used Chancellor Claude Fletcher to help raise millions of dollars, the gym logos are beautiful and the sound in our stadiums could not be better.

18. No Secrets

Always share the vision that God gives to you with those who will listen. On more than one occasion I have shared God's vision with people of seemingly modest means that eventually gave tens of thousands or millions of dollars in response to God's leading. Be faithful to share the vision but understand that it is only God who can lead people to give their time, talent and treasure from their hearts.

19. Aim For The Stars

Aim for excellence in everything you do. Understand that, ultimately, true excellence is the nature, character, and works of God. Anything we do that truly reflects excellence requires the work of God and is by definition "supernatural." Pursuing His excellence opens the door to experiencing His supernatural activity in your everyday life—naturally.

20. Journal The Journey

Periodically document the ways God has supernaturally worked through your life. Honor Him for His faithfulness, and allow these accounts to bring you and others into a new dimension of faith and love of God.

CHAPTER 23
MUSTARD SEED OR POTATO FAITH?

While praying that God would build the Skyway campus I thought of Jesus' words, " . . . assuredly, I say to you, if you have faith as a mustard seed, you will say to this mountain, 'Move from here to there,' and it will move; and nothing will be impossible for you" (Matthew 17:20). I learned from our engineers that, except for the area around the oak tree on the northeast side of the campus, every part of the Skyway "mountain" would be moved to build Skyway campus. Some interesting facts include:

- The top of the crest where we needed to place the baseball field was so narrow that I had to drive nearly all the way to San Ramon Drive on the west side of the property to turn around. The alternative was to risk falling over the side of steep 300-foot drop-offs.
- The south side of the campus was too steep to build a road. A 1250-foot wall rises to about 40 feet at its highest point to support the entry road to the campus, Skyway Drive. The road was built with dirt and rock that came from the baseball field.
- About one third of the dirt and rock for the football field came from other portions of the "mountain" and is retained by an 80 foot high retaining wall system.
- Every athletic field, the pool and all four buildings required large "cut outs" and retaining walls to create level spaces for construction.
- Most of the hill is composed of serpentine rock. Almost 600,000 cubic yards of rock was broken into

gravel by large equipment and rock crushers to use as fill to make the athletic fields, building pads and roads.

Just to move 600,000 cubic yards of crushed rock and dirt required 40,000 double trailer dump truck loads. They carried about 15 cubic yards per trip.

Obviously, I pondered, *we need mustard seed faith to move the Skyway Mountain for construction of the school!*

So I, like the apostles, asked Jesus to "increase" my faith. I wondered what was so special about the mustard seed. Jesus said that this seed " . . . is the smallest of all seeds, but it becomes the largest of garden plants and grows into a tree where birds can come and find shelter in its branches" (Matthew 13:32 NLT).

I wondered, "*What is it about the mustard seed compared to say a potato seed that prompted Jesus use it to illustrate mountain moving faith?*"

Some thoughts about mustard seed faith came to me.

1. Although the mustard seed is very small it contains a complete set of God's plans to grow a small tree that is larger than all the plants of the garden as a home for birds.

   I felt small and inadequate to build the school. I had no options but to stand on Christ's promise that if we would "seek first the Kingdom of God and His righteousness," He would add all that we needed to build the school. His promise proved true. He provided all that we needed including His goodness, His desires, His vision, His plans, His works and His resources. I held tight to God's admonition and promise, "Delight yourself also in the Lord, and He shall give you the desires of your heart" (Psalm 37:4). This promise is so powerful because of its double meaning. If we delight ourselves in the Lord, God will place His desires (vision/plans/passion) in our hearts and then He will bring them to pass.

Although the mustard seed is so small, it contains all of the elements and plans of a large tree in miniature form. With this example of the mustard seed, I became passionate about making sure that the school's building plans were complete in that they included every imaginable "part" needed to grow a comprehensive Quest for Excellence™ Christian school. It's important that, like the mustard seed, we must get God's plans from the drawing room of heaven. We should never settle for something less. My best plans made on earth or my plans for something small we can afford to build, will never match God's plans. A great indicator as to whether we have God's plans is that God's plans are always larger than our biggest dreams, and they seemingly always cost many times more than we could ever manage without God's supernatural help.

2. Compared to the potato, the mustard seed is so small that it has only enough resources to start its tree-growing project but not nearly enough resources to actually grow the tree. In other words, the mustard seed has a huge project deficit.

Like the mustard seed, we barely had enough resources to plan the school but we had no money to even begin construction. In fact, it was a challenge to get together enough money to pay the architects, engineers, the environmental engineers and our project planners. So, just as a mustard seed has only enough resources to make the first push through the soil, we scraped up just enough money to pay for the planning of the school. I learned the importance of the Lord's admonition to Zerubbabel. "Do not despise these small beginnings, for the Lord rejoices to see the work begin, to see the plumb line in Zerubbabel's hand" (Zechariah 4:10 NLT).

I cannot deny that at times I questioned, "Lord, if we are having trouble paying thousands of dollars for planning the school, how will we find tens of millions of dollars to build the school?" But I heard the Lord's confident assurance in my heart, "You start like the mustard seed, and I'll finish like God Almighty." As a result of God's encouragement, like the mustard seed, we did not despair because of what appeared to be an impossible project deficit. When we planned the school "according to God's high standards" He gave us the gift of mustard seed faith to believe that He would cover our project deficit and finish the school.

3. The mustard seed, unlike the potato seed, must immediately tap into resources outside of itself or die.

Have you ever seen a forgotten potato? It begins to grow long roots with its own potato resources. Compared to the mustard seed, the potato provides vast resources for its seed to sprout and grow. It can grow long vines without exposure to light, moisture or soil.

What a contrast to the mustard seed. With only enough resources for one push to start, the mustard seed must immediately tap into resources outside of itself after its first and only push.

Without doubt, as Christians, we must have faith like a mustard seed to accomplish what only God can do. The lesson is simple but profound. If we allow ourselves to become the repository of God's plans, and agree to passionately follow His vision, He will do His great works through our hands. The bonus is that He takes care of our project deficit with His resources. Like the mustard seed, we have only enough strength to document His plans and to begin the project. Only God can grow a mustard tree. Fortunately, God's vision is never lacking His provision!

It is tempting to want to be more like a potato seed than like mustard seed. The potato could easily be deceived into thinking that it has all the resources needed to grow more potatoes. What a trap! In spite of all its resources, like the mustard seed, the potato needs light, moisture, and soil or it too must die.

Jesus says that we need mustard seed faith to move mountains and that nothing is impossible to those who have it. In short, the mustard seed has God's plans, spends all of its limited resources to start and immediately taps into God's resources outside of itself to complete its God-ordained purpose to grow a mustard tree. We should all pray to have the wisdom, courage and determination of the mustard seed in the face of insurmountable tasks and limited resources. God's will can only to be accomplished by His grace and strength alone and not our own. May we never seek to be like a deluded potato seed that thinks it has all the resources needed to grow potatoes.

To summarize, the mustard seed knows of three certainties:

- It has a God-given purpose, plan and passion to grow a mustard tree as a lodging place for birds.
- It has only enough resources to begin growing a tree but far from enough to finish.
- It begins to grow a tree with all of the strength it has and reaches outside of itself for the needed God-given resources to finish the job.

May we all have mustard seed faith!

"God opposes the proud but gives grace to the humble." Humble yourselves, therefore, under God's mighty hand, that He may lift you up in due time. Cast all your anxiety on Him because He cares for you" (1 Peter 5:5–7 NIV).

CONTACT INFORMATION
If you are interested in learning more about the Quest for Excellence™ in your professional sphere of influence, contact:

The Quest Institute for Christian Schools™
Quest@ValleyChristian.net
100 Skyway Drive
San Jose CA 95111
408–513–2500

THE ENEMY OF FAITH IS NOT UNBELIEF BUT MEMORY
(BY ED SILVOSO)

God has far more faith in you than any amount of faith you may possibly have in Him.

When it comes to faith we are fruitlessly self-centered and end up being limited by our own lack of faith because our faith is rooted in our own capacity to believe. But Christianity is not about us, but about God, and God has unlimited faith in us because He sees us through the lens of a bright future dotted with myriads of victories still to be accomplished instead of the failures marking our past.

The enemy of faith is not so much unbelief as it is memory because memory is the record of what has already taken place whereas faith is the revelation of what is yet to happen.

This is vividly illustrated in the Great Commission (Matthew 28:18–20) where Jesus told His disciples to disciple, teach and baptize not just one, but all the nations. Traditionally we interpret this to mean that Jesus sent us to make individual disciples, something that is true in the general body of New Testament truth, but definitely not the main point in this passage. Here Jesus states unequivocally that we are to disciple, teach and baptize nations.

This becomes more perplexing when we realize that this command was first given to people who until then had never traveled outside of Palestine, to folks profoundly Jewish who viewed the world through an extremely confining, self-centered, nationalistic perspective. Nevertheless Jesus, with unlimited faith in them, announced that they would reach the end of the earth to disciple nations.

We know that they succeeded because in Revelation 21:24–27 we read that nations and their rulers will bring the honor and the glory of those nations to God, in a sublime climax when nation after nation, representing millions of people whose names are written in the Lamb's Book of Life, will parade before God as evidence that they have been discipled, baptized and taught as per Jesus' instructions.

This is why it is so important to realize that this is not about us but about God. It is not what we think that counts but what He says. It is not our plan but His plan, not our faith but His faith.

The issue of faith, and particularly how much faith God has in us, is eloquently illustrated by the story of Gideon (Judges, Chapters 6–8). Usually when we think of Gideon we picture a brave, fearless man who knew nothing but an unending string of victories.

However, Gideon lived at a time of total desolation for his nation and for him personally as well. Year after year, when harvest time came and God's people were ready to enjoy the fruit of their labors, their enemies descended on Israel like locusts taking over its fields and vineyards, slaughtering its animals and literally raping the land—in essence, devastating the nation unobstructed while God's people hid in caves in nearby hills from where they watched their foes plunder the fruit of their labors.

On one such occasion Gideon was concealing wheat seeds in the wine cellar before taking off to hide in a cave to watch his fields as his enemies destroyed them. Gideon was not planning to fight, not even to passively resist the invaders. He was overwhelmed by fear and impotence and, as a result, was hiding some grain so that when he came down from the cave after witnessing the devastation of his fields he would have something with which to plant a new crop so that the following year his enemies would have something else to steal from him. Not a very uplifting picture.

It is at this juncture that an angel visits him to declare: "The Lord is with you, mighty warrior" (Judges 6:12). This is a strange salutation because it does not appear to be accurate since Gideon was not a warrior—he was a fleeing civilian—and by no stretch of the imagination could he be considered mighty. On the contrary, he was a defeated man, crushed inside and devoid of hope. But we know that angels cannot lie, they are sinless and they always deliver messages from God. So, it is correct to assume that the statement that Gideon was a mighty warrior originated with God. Can God lie? Of course not! Then how can this statement, so at odds with reality, be true?

The reason why Gideon could be truthfully called a mighty warrior is because God has a better opinion of us than the opinion we have of ourselves. God's opinion is determined by future victories, still unseen, whereas our concept of our self and our capability (or lack of) is determined by failures in our past.

God was able to see Gideon as he was going to be and not the way he was at the time he was gutlessly hiding grain in a wine cellar.

This is also true of you. Today you need to make a decision: Whose report will you believe? God's or the enemy's? This is why I said earlier that the enemy of faith is not so much unbelief as it is memory, because the latter reminds us of what we have seen, whereas the former reveals what is yet to be seen.

Gideon, obviously, was not convinced that God

was with him and much less that he was a mighty warrior. That is why he went on to argue with the angel, challenging him that if God was indeed with him, why hadn't he seen the miracles that his forefathers talked so much about.

"Why" is the devil's favorite question because only God can fully answer it since the answer requires command of all facts and variables? When facing a crisis, either personally or institutionally, asking why things happened, or did not happen, drives us deeper into despair. The moment we focus on this question we begin to doubt the power of God and the reality of miracles. This is how Gideon ended up questioning if the miracles he heard so much about really happened.

It is very revealing that next God himself replaced the angel. I can imagine God saying to Gabriel, "Move over. This is a tough case that requires my personal attention." The Lord, instead of answering Gideon's question, went on to give him a most improbable assignment: "On this your strength, go and save the nation." I say improbable, humanly speaking, because Gideon had hardly any strength, and whatever strength he had was not adequate to save himself, much less the nation.

But there is a powerful principle at work here. God is telling Gideon, "Forget about yourself and focus on the purpose for which you are created. Stop thinking about mere personal survival and trust Me for something that will change everything around you."

While VCS was focused on mere survival, struggling to come up with well meaning, albeit temporary, short-serving solutions, its destiny was never addressed. Saving a nation, or a school, requires total dependence on God and the reception of new ideas, new power, new anointing. This is why you need to believe God's report instead of the sum of your own fears and doubts. God has a very positive opinion of you and He is commanding you to shift from survival to an overcoming mode. Go for the transformation of your sphere of influence in the market-place and not merely for solving today's crisis.

Next, God instructed Gideon to go to his father's house to tear down the altar of Baal and the image of Ash-era adjacent to it, and to use the wood from the latter to build an altar to the Lord on which to sacrifice Gideon's dad's prized bulls.

Gideon was again consumed by fear and deeply rooted feelings of incompetence because he was the youngest in his father's household and his own family was not a prominent one in Israel. He knew that the moment the altars were torn down the elders of the city would put pressure on his dad and Gideon's hide would be publicly tanned.

But in spite of his fears he chose to obey, although he did not carry out the assignment in the daytime because he was too afraid for that. Instead he did it at night when no one was watching. The next morning, when the elders found the altars missing, they determined in no time that it was the work of Gideon and decided to report it to his father, knowing that he would not be very happy to find out that two of his prize bulls were destroyed as well. All of Gideon's fears were about to come to pass. He knew that he held the lowest ranking in his family and also that his father's household was not a prominent one, having no pull against the enraged city elders.

But against all odds, Gideon's father took sides with him and told the elders, mockingly, that if Baal had an issue with his son the idol should take it up directly with Gideon. In fact, Gideon's dad became so proud of Gideon's actions that he changed his name to Jerubaal, which basically means, "The one who contends with Baal."

Why such a dramatic turn of events? Here we find the second principle. Not only does God have a better opinion of you than you have of yourself, but when you agree to shift from survival to overcoming mode, He will cause your friends to develop a better opinion of you than you think is possible.

So many Christians, including school administrators, are pinned down in their faith by what their board members, associates, family and friends think, or what they think they might think or do. Memory, especially the memory of past failures, has erected altars of impotence on the hills surrounding the valley of helplessness where they labor in despair. When they try to lift their eyes to the Lord, they cannot get past those hills dotted with so many memorials enshrining old setbacks.

It is about time that you choose to obey God, even if you are afraid and need to do it at night, so to speak, but do it. Tear down the strongholds that are perpetuating failure in your work and ministry by imposing a ceiling on what God can do. After looking at things with the eyes of the Spirit and discerning God's purposes and plans, you need to declare it before your elders and your peers. You must proclaim the word of the Lord and stand on that challenging threshold framed by fear on one side and faith on the other and tell your family and friends that you have chosen to stand on the side of faith because God said so, even though in the natural it looks impossible.

You will be surprised by the unexpected results once you tear down those altars because it is impossible for others to develop faith while living in the shadow of altars to failure. Someone has to speak the word of the Lord for Him to confirm it because He will not confirm it unless you speak it up first. Do not be afraid of man but go ahead and declare the word of the Lord.

Once Gideon's self image and the opinion of his elders had been reshaped in God's will, God instructed him to go to the enemy's camp to discover how victory would be obtained. What God told Gideon, a perennial worrier, is almost comical because God proposed that if Gideon was afraid to go down by himself he could take his servant Purah. This seems like a touch of divine humor - Gideon's enemies numbered in the hundreds of thousands. What difference would it make if Gideon went by himself or with another person? One or two people facing half a million barbarians make no difference. What we know is that Gideon, being afraid, decided to bring his servant along.

Upon arriving in the enemy's camp, in the dead of night and in total darkness, Gideon became privy to a conversation going on inside one of the tents. Someone was relating a dream in which he saw a loaf of bread blow into the camp and strike the main tent, causing it to collapse. His interlocutor immediately provided an interpretation that I am sure surprised Gideon more than anyone else when he heard the statement: "This is no other than Gideon, into whose hands God has delivered us." And this is exactly what happened.

And here is the third principle: not only does God have a better opinion of you than you have of yourself, and He will cause your friends and family to think better of you than you think is possible, but God will make your enemies have a better opinion of you!

God has already decreed victory for those that walk with Him. Jesus stated unequivocally that the Gates of Hades will not prevail against us. This is a given. But for this to happen, in our sphere of influence, we need to move from survival to overcoming, from mediocrity to excellence, from the natural to the supernatural. We need to leave the wine cellar where we hope to achieve temporary survival and fight for our nation, for our destiny. We must stop looking down and instead lift up our eyes to the One who made the heavens and the earth.

To be able to do this effectively the first step is to eliminate the memory of past failures and limitations as the determining factor of what we can actually trust God for. You must believe God when He says that greater is He who is in you than the one who is in the world causing spiritual mischief (I John 4:4). It is not enough to believe in God. You must now believe God!

The second step is to declare the word of the Lord to those in your inner circle—family, friends and peers. It is not enough to believe something in your heart. It needs to pass through your lips as a declaration of faith. This is what Paul teaches in Romans when he states that what we believe in our heart and confess with our mouth is counted as righteousness. Speak the word of the Lord and wait for Him to confirm it in the hearts of your co-laborers, but do not waiver. God is already at work in their lives. Rest assured that when God spoke to Cornelius about Peter, He also spoke to Peter about Cornelius, but nothing of consequence happened until those two took the risk and met in unusual and challenging circumstances (see full story in Acts 10).

And finally, be encouraged knowing that God has already declared to the forces of evil bent on destroying your dreams and devouring the fruit of your labors that they will be defeated by you. God has faith in you because He lives in you! Now you need to come out of the cave and invade the enemy's camp. Even if you are afraid, you need to take the fight to the enemy. As you do it you will be pleasantly surprised to find evidence that God has already made provision for victory.

Isaiah 43:18 cautions us not to bring to mind things of the past but to be aware that God is doing a new thing. And because He is doing something new you need to understand that your fight now is not so much with the devil as it is with yourself and with your old beliefs, or disbeliefs. And in such context the enemy of your faith becomes your memory, the memory of past failures and limitations. This is why right now you need to let the Spirit of God come upon you to lift you up to new heights from where you will be able to see what God has in store. Don't be afraid of the new because if you want to see what you have never seen, you will have to do what you have never done, because if you continue doing what you always do, you will continue to see what you always see.

This book has undoubtedly inspired you and it has filled your soul with faith. Faith is powerful, but faith can be killed by just one thing—lack of works—since the Bible teaches that faith without works is dead. No matter how tiny your faith is today, if you put it to work it will grow, but if you don't, it will die. Put it to work and do not despise small beginnings because what is from God is bound to grow.

This is why I say to you, in the name of Jesus, mighty warrior, arise and build because the Lord is with you!

ABOUT THE AUTHOR

Dr. Cliff Daugherty joined Valley Christian Schools as President/Superintendent in July 1986. Under his leadership, enrollment has more than doubled and permanent facilities were constructed for all three campuses with a current value of more than $100 million. He is the Founder of Neighborhood Christian Preschools, the Christian Schools Association of Santa Clara County and the Quest Institute for Christian Education and served as the founding principal of Los Altos Christian Schools. Dr. Daugherty received his B.S. in English Literature, Bible and Theology from Bethany College, his M.A. in Public School Administration from San Jose State University and his Ed.D. in Private School Administration and Special Education from the University of San Francisco. He holds lifetime California and ACSI Teaching and Administrative credentials. Dr. Daugherty and his wife, Kris, live in San Jose, California. They have two children and three grandchildren.

CONTRIBUTING WRITER OF THE FOREWORD, CHAPTER 17 AND THE ADDENDUM

Ed Silvoso is the founder and president of Harvest Evangelism and the International Transformation Network. His scriptural insights on the role of Christians in the marketplace and his biblically based strategies on how to take the presence and power of God to the workplace have enabled multitudes of business people to find their spiritual destiny by turning their jobs into their ministry. Ed's best-selling books include *That None Should Perish, Prayer Evangelism, Women–God's Secret Weapon* and, more recently, his groundbreaking book *Anointed for Business*. www.harvestevan.org

(ENDNOTES)

[1] Later, in the summer of 2004, the Smith family elected to sell their home to VCS for a reduced price and move to Colorado. As it turned out, home values did increase dramatically after the school was built, but Dan and Janet felt that their children received the greater value by attending Valley Christian Schools.

[2] South Valley Christian Church had not begun building on their portion of the hill; at this writing that land remains undeveloped.

[3] Valley Christian School's tuition assistance program

[4] Based on ten months of salary; teachers could elect to have their annual salary paid over ten, eleven or twelve months' pay periods.

[5] A competency-based teacher compensation plan was implemented for the 2005–2006 school year. Valley's five-year plan calls for a forty-two percent increase in teacher salaries. It is expected that the school will tile the stairs when VCS teachers are among the best-paid teachers in the nation.

TATE PUBLISHING & *Enterprises*

Tate Publishing is commited to excellence in the publishing industry. Our staff of highly trained professionals, including editors, graphic designers, and marketing personnel, work together to produce the very finest books available. The company reflects the philosophy established by the founders, based on Psalms 68:11,

"THE LORD GAVE THE WORD AND GREAT WAS THE COMPANY OF THOSE WHO PUBLISHED IT."

If you would like further information, please call
1.888.361.9473
or visit our website
www.tatepublishing.com

TATE PUBLISHING & *Enterprises*, LLC
127 E. Trade Center Terrace
Mustang, Oklahoma 73064 USA